Ghostly Frequencies

Ghostly Frequencies

THE PHYSICS OF SPIRITS

HURMUZ AIN

Spectra Enterprise

Contents

INDEX

Chapter 7: Interdimensional Physics: Bridging the Gap Between Realms

INTRODUCTION

Since the beginning of human history, the idea of ghosts and spirits has been a vital component of human culture and tradition. Despite the fact that it is sometimes disregarded as nothing more than superstition, the concept of spectral entities residing in a realm that is beyond our comprehension continues to be prevalent in a variety of nations and belief systems. Over the past few years, there has been an increasing interest in investigating the phenomenon of ghosts from a scientific point of view, with the goal of attempting to comprehend the physical principles that are responsible for these said apparitions. With the goal of elucidating the unexplained relationship that exists between the physical and metaphysical realms, this investigation goes into the domain of ghostly vibrations.

Perspectives on the Past: historic

In order to properly understand the scientific elements of ghosts and spirits, it is necessary to first accept the historical viewpoints that have had a role in shaping the perception of these entities. Throughout the course of human history, diverse cultures have provided a wide range of interpretations of these ethereal entities. The human experience has been braided with stories of encounters with ghosts from ancient civilizations to modern society. These stories have been passed down from generation to generation. These tales frequently contain recurring motifs, such as apparitions, voices that are not embodied, and happenings that cannot be explained, all of which hint at the existence of a spectral presence that is beyond the comprehension of the living.

An Overview of the Transition to Scientific Inquiry:

In the process of the scientific method becoming the preeminent technique to comprehending the world, the research of paranormal events was sometimes relegated to the background or disregarded entirely. In spite of this, scientists and researchers have begun to investigate the prospect of explaining ghostly phenomena via the lens of physics. This is not just due to developments in technology, but also to a more open-minded approach to unorthodox themes.

Fields of Electromagnetic Energy and Other Dimensional Manifestations:

The investigation of electromagnetic fields (EMFs) is a fascinating route that might be pursued in the pursuit of gaining an understanding of the physical properties of spirits. Different natural and man-made sources are responsible for the generation of electromagnetic fields, which can be found everywhere. According to the hypothesis of a few studies, ghosts could be able to interact with these fields and manipulate them in order to present themselves or converse with live people.

The electromagnetic field that is produced by the human body is rather modest but can nevertheless be detected. The movement of charged particles within the body and the electrical activity that occurs in the nervous system are the two factors that contribute to the formation of this field. According to proponents of the electromagnetic hypothesis of ghosts, after a person passes away, the energy that once animated the body may continue to exist and interact with the electromagnetic environment that is all around them.

In order to identify oscillations in electromagnetic fields, paranormal investigations frequently make use of instruments such as electromagnetic field meters (EMF meters). The presence of a ghostly being may be indicated by spikes in these readings, according to the argument of certain individuals. Skeptics, on the other hand, argue that changes in electromagnetic fields (EMF) can be caused by a variety of everyday causes, such as electrical appliances or wiring. This has led to a discussion among the scientific community regarding the legitimacy of utilizing EMF measurements as evidence of paranormal activity.

In addition to Ghostly Frequencies, Resonance:

In the context of ghostly frequencies, another idea that is investigated is resonance, which refers to the phenomena in which an object vibrates at a particular frequency when it is subjected to vibrations from the outside. According to this theory, spirits may be able to resonate with particular frequencies, which would enable them to interact with the physical world or become detectable to those who are still alive.

Taking this line of reasoning into consideration, it is possible that particular environmental conditions or energy patterns could set off resonant responses from residual energies or beings. It has been suggested by researchers that gaining an understanding of the resonance frequencies that are connected with ghostly manifestations could present opportunities for conducting tests that are more controlled and could potentially lead to the creation of devices that can detect or perhaps converse with spirits.

A Discussion of Parallel Realities and Quantum Mechanics

Taking a step into the realm of speculation, there are scholars who have proposed that there are linkages between spectral phenomena and the fundamental principles of quantum physics. Concepts like superposition and entanglement are introduced in quantum mechanics, which is a branch of physics that deals with the behavior of sub-atomic particles. These concepts present a challenge to our traditional view of reality.

The existence of ghosts in a parallel realm or dimension that occasionally connects with our own is a hypothesis that has been put up.

In accordance with this theory, the physical principles that control these parallel realms might make it possible for the living and the dead to engage in fleeting contacts with one another briefly. In spite of the fact that it is intriguing, this idea is highly hypothetical and does not have any scientific proof to back it up, which is why many scientists approach it with caution.

Aspects of the psychological and perceptual nature:

It is essential to take into consideration the role that psychology and perception play in ghostly encounters, in addition to investigating the physical phenomena that are involved. The human mind is likely to be subject to a variety of cognitive biases and perceptual errors, both of which have the potential to contribute to the experience of paranormal activity.

The necessity of knowing the function that the human mind plays in processing ambiguous stimuli is frequently emphasized by parapsychologists and psychologists who investigate paranormal experiences. The manner in which individuals understand and recall their experiences with the supernatural can be profoundly influenced by a variety of factors, including cultural influences, belief systems, and the influence of suggestion.

The Function of Technology in the Investigation of Paranormal Occurrences:

There has been a considerable impact that technological advancements have had on the way that current paranormal investigations are conducted. For the purpose of gathering evidence of supernatural activity, ghost hunters and other aficionados of the paranormal frequently make use of a wide range of tools and machines. Infra-red cameras and digital voice recorders are examples of the types of technology that are utilized for the purpose of documenting abnormalities that may represent the existence of ghosts.

It is a gadget that rapidly scans radio frequencies, producing white noise and enables users to interpret probable spirit communication in the random audio snippets. The spirit box, also known as the ghost box, is one of the tools that is extensively utilized. Skeptics contend that pareidolia, which is the tendency of the human mind to recognize familiar patterns in random stimuli, may be at play, despite the fact that some people claim to have successfully communicated with spirits using these devices.

Skepticism and Obstacles on the Path:

In spite of the fact that research into the physics of spirits is still being conducted, the area continues to be fraught with controversy and to be met with a significant amount of skepticism from the scientific world. There are a number of experts that say that it is difficult to establish a scientific basis for the presence of ghosts since there is a lack of evidence that can be reproduced and verified, in addition to the influence of psychological and perceptual elements.

The cultural and historical context around ghostly events is another topic of contention among critics. They argue that the belief in ghosts is frequently strongly founded in the cultural traditions and religious beliefs of a variety of different cultures. As a consequence of this, the interpretation of paranormal experiences may frequently be highly influenced by cultural frameworks that have already been established.

There is a fascinating convergence of science, folklore, and the inexplicable that may be found in the investigation of haunting frequencies and the physics of spirits.

Although there has been a rise in interest in understanding paranormal events as a result of technological advancements and a more open-minded approach to scientific inquiry, the topic continues to be riddled with difficulties and mistrust.

The investigation into the mysteries of ghosts continues, regardless of whether the source of the riddles lies in electromagnetic fields, resonance, quantum mechanics, or psychological variables. As scientific approaches and technological advancements continue to progress, it is possible that researchers will obtain fresh insights into the nature of these elusive entities. Until that day comes, the physics of spirits will continue to be a fascinating and mysterious domain that offers opportunities for more inquiry and thought.

Chapter 1

Introduction: Unveiling the Unseen Realm

Over the course of human history, the mysteries that lie beyond the curtain of our everyday perception have never failed to capture the interest of humans. As we strive to comprehend the cosmos and our position within it, we find ourselves pulled to the mysterious, the unknowable, and the unseen. The concept of an unseen dimension that exists in parallel with our actual reality has been a recurrent subject over the course of human history, transcending distinctions between cultures, religions, and philosophical schools of thought. This investigation digs into the myriad of facets that make up the unseen realm. It investigates the realms of physics, metaphysics, spirituality, and the human mind in order to uncover the layers of reality that are hidden from our ordinary senses.

This is the historical tapestry that is rarely seen:

The idea of an unseen realm is deeply ingrained in the fabric of human history, and it has taken on a variety of forms across the various cultures and civilizations that have existed throughout the course of human history. Throughout the history of mythology, gods, spirits, and other supernatural beings frequently inhabited regions that were beyond the comprehension of mortals. These unseen dimensions were portrayed as locations of immense power, mystery, and occasionally risk, and the only people who could reach them were those who possessed special powers or was blessed by the divine.

At certain times or places, it was believed that the veil that between the visible and the invisible was thin, which made it possible for the divine and the mortal to communicate with one another or interact with one another. Many ancient societies had rituals, rites, and practices that were aimed at shattering this veil. These practices and rituals reflected a deep-seated human need to connect with energies that are beyond the grasp of ordinary senses.

Concepts of the Unseen from a Religious Perspective:

Since ancient times, religious traditions all over the world have stated the presence of unseen realms that are inhabited by various spiritual creatures such as deities, angels, demons, and other spiritual beings. Scripture in Christianity makes references to celestial regions and spiritual battle, putting an emphasis on the cosmic conflict between forces that can be seen and those that cannot be seen.

The religion of Islam references the existence of jinn, which are beings that are created from smokeless fire and coexist with people in a dimension that is beyond the realm of ordinary perception.

The religions of Buddhism and Hinduism both dig into complex cosmologies that consist of several worlds and dimensions, with each realm and dimension housing a different set of gods, heavenly beings, and enlightened entities. According to these Eastern philosophies, the interconnection of life, death, and rebirth suggests that one must experience a continual journey through both visible and invisible states of existence.

Unseen in Philosophy: What Is It?

Philosophers, like everyone else, have struggled with the idea of the realm that cannot be seen. Plato's Allegory of the Cave, for example, investigates the concept that our vision of reality is analogous to shadows on the wall of a cave, and that genuine knowledge lies beyond what is immediately visible. Immanuel Kant, a philosopher, put out the idea that there are noumena, which are things that exist independently of human sensory experience and are beyond the sphere of human comprehension.

Unseen in the Field of Physics:

In tandem with the development of our comprehension of the material world, our understanding of the invisible has also progressed. The basic conceptions that we have of the components that make up the universe are being called into question by occurrences in the field of physics, such as dark matter and dark energy. The gravitational effects of dark matter are felt, despite the fact that it does not emit, absorb, or reflect light. Dark matter continues to be elusive and incapable of being detected by traditional methods.

In a similar vein, the enigmatic element known as dark energy, which is responsible for the accelerating expansion of the universe, is completely beyond our ability to directly observe. The dimensions of the universe that cannot be seen, which are inferred through mathematical models and data gathered from observations, provide a clue at a vast and hidden element of reality that is incompatible with our senses and the conventional scientific procedures.

In the field of physics, string theory and quantum mechanics are considered to be cutting-edge fields since they introduce the idea of other dimensions and parallel worlds living alongside our own Universe. Our intuition is put to the test and the boundaries of what we assume to be real and visible are pushed farther by these ideas, which postulate the existence of unseen realms that are governed by specific physical characteristics.

Investigations into the Metaphysical:

Extending beyond the domain of science, metaphysical traditions and esoteric ideologies postulate the presence of unseen energies, auras, and subtle realms that have an effect on our physical reality. Meditation, energy healing, and divination are all examples of practices that frequently require an awareness of these energy forces that cannot be seen. The concept of auras, for example, posits that humans emanate delicate energy fields that can be experienced by those with heightened sensory capacities.

The term "chakra" originates from Eastern traditions and refers to energy centers that are located within the body. Each chakra is connected with a distinct set of characteristics and perspectives on consciousness. It is believed that the invisible flow of energy through these centers contributes to the well-being of the spiritual, mental, and bodily aspects of this individual.

Psychic phenomena, telepathy, and clairvoyance are frequently attributed to the capacity to access the invisible dimensions of consciousness. Clarity of vision is another common quality. In the event that they are genuine, psychic experiences provide evidence that the mind is capable of going beyond the constraints of the physical senses and providing glimpses into realms that are beyond the sphere of regular perception.

The Unseen in the Spirituality of the Contemporary Era:

There are many different ways that the investigation of the unseen realm has been carried out in the current spiritual environment. Ancient knowledge, esoteric rituals, and a synthesis of Eastern and Western spiritual beliefs are all components of New Age movements, which aim to provide a more comprehensive understanding of the world around us. There is a strong connection between the visible and invisible parts of existence, which is highlighted by ideas such as the law of attraction, energy healing, and the power of intention.

As a result of individuals asserting that they have the capacity to bridge the gap between the living and the deceased, there has been a rise in interest in mediumship and communication with the spirit realm. Channeling sessions, séances, and spirit guides are all methods that some people use in order to gain access to knowledge that is supposedly from the realms that cannot be seen.

A Look at the Part That Technology Plays in Revealing the Unseen:

These days, technology has evolved into a tool that may reveal things that were previously hidden from view in ways that our forefathers could not have imagined. Telescopes are able to see into the depths of the universe, displaying celestial events that are beyond the span of human vision when it is not surrounded by a telescope.

Microscopes shed light on the complexities of the world that exist on a tiny scale, where life thrives in dimensions that are not visible to the naked eye.

When it comes to the domain of the paranormal, technology is frequently utilized in order to record and investigate things that cannot be seen. Infrared cameras are able to capture images that extend beyond the visible light spectrum, which has the potential to reveal things or energies that are beyond the range of our typical perception. Recordings of electronic voice phenomena (EVP) are made with the intention of capturing voices or noises from the spirit world that may be inaudible to the human ear.

The technologies of augmented reality (AR) and virtual reality (VR) provide immersive experiences that replicate invisible realms. These technologies allow a glimpse into fanciful landscapes or spiritual dimensions from the perspective of the user. Despite the fact that these technical breakthroughs do not necessarily prove the existence of supernatural worlds, they do reflect humanity's persistent curiosity with the unseen and our creative efforts to investigate it.

Skepticism and Obstacles on the Path:

In spite of the fact that people have always been fascinated by things that cannot be seen, the concept is met with opposition and doubt from a variety of sources. The scientific method is a method that is used in the field of science. It requires empirical facts and hypotheses that can be tested. The repeatability and verifiability that are necessary to establish claims of paranormal or supernatural occurrences as scientific facts are frequently lacking in the reports of such phenomena.

Some people believe that many of the reported encounters with the unseen can be traced to psychological variables such as suggestion, cognitive biases, and the power of the imagination. Skeptics contend that this is all possible. The tendency of the human mind to look for patterns and significance in randomness is referred to as pareidolia, and it may be one of the factors that contributes to the sense of supernatural happenings in situations when none actually exist.

It is also important to note that cultural and religious circumstances play a crucial impact in the formation of beliefs regarding the unseen. It is possible that what one culture considers to be proof of the supernatural could be seen differently by another society or religious system depending on the context. The subjective and culturally conditioned nature of these interpretations is brought into focus by the wide variety of beliefs that surround the unseen realm.

As a reflection of humanity's never-ending search for comprehension and significance, the investigation of the unseen realm encompasses not only the realms of history and spirituality but also those of science and philosophy. As a thread that connects all elements of the human experience, the concept of the unseen continues to be present, whether it is through ancient mythology, religious tales, scientific study, or current spiritual activities.

Despite the fact that we are currently standing at the crossroads of old knowledge and contemporary technology, the expedition to reveal the hidden continues. We are compelled to tackle the mysteries of the unseen realm with intellectual rigor and an openness to the unknown because of the hurdles and skepticism that surround this pursuit. From the perspective of the unfolding story of human exploration, the unseen realm continues to be a tempting frontier, inviting us to look beyond the veil and explore the limitless possibilities that lie just beyond our typical perception.

1.1 Setting the stage for scientific exploration of the paranormal

When it comes to the junction of science and the paranormal, there has always been a great deal of dispute, skepticism, and mystery surrounding this very area. In contrast to the standard scientific approaches, which place a strong emphasis on empirical evidence and repeatability, the paranormal frequently deals with events that are difficult to measure or explain. The voyage to investigate the paranormal through the application of rigorous scientific methods has been undertaken by an increasing number of scientists and researchers, despite the difficulties that have been encountered. This investigation lays the groundwork for a nuanced and open-minded investigation of the unexplained, with a particular focus on the scientific method, technological advancements, and the combined efforts of researchers from many fields.

The Obstacles That Stand in the Way of Scientifically Investigating the Paranormal:

The scientific investigation of the supernatural is fraught with difficulties, the most significant of which originate from the elusive and frequently subjective nature of the phenomena that are considered to be supernatural. In contrast to controlled laboratory experiments, paranormal occurrences are frequently unplanned, transient, and impossible to replicate under controlled conditions. Additionally, because of the subjective character of personal experiences, it is difficult to construct a framework that is widely accepted for the study of the paranormal.

Some people believe that many claims about the paranormal are founded on cognitive biases, perceptual errors, and the human predisposition to look for patterns and significance in random information. Skeptics put up this argument. Researchers who want to bring scientific rigor to the study of the paranormal face considerable challenges as a result of these circumstances.

What Has Happened to Parapsychology Over Time?

The area of parapsychology, which is devoted to the scientific investigation of paranormal events, came into existence in the latter half of the 19th century as a reaction to the growing interest of the general public in spiritual philosophy and the supernatural. Experimental investigations into extrasensory perception (ESP) and psychokinesis (PK) were carried out in a controlled laboratory environment by early parapsychologists such as Joseph B. Rhine. Even though their work was crucial in laying the groundwork for the scientific investigation of the supernatural, it was also subject to criticism for having methodological problems and contradictions.

In the course of the development of parapsychology, researchers endeavored to improve experimental protocols and respond to criticisms from the other members of the scientific community. When it comes to analyzing and interpreting the outcomes of experiments, the utilization of statistical tools, randomized control trials, and meta-analyses have become common practices. In spite of these attempts, parapsychology remained to live on the periphery of mainstream science, and a significant number of scientists continued to be dubious of the claims that it puts up.

Technology and instrumentation advancements include the following:

The transformation of the scientific investigation of the supernatural has been significantly influenced by the development of new technologies. Researchers in the modern day have access to a vast array of technologies and devices that make it possible for them to collect data and evidence in ways that were previously impossible.

When conducting investigations into the paranormal, it is common practice to make use of electromagnetic field (EMF) meters, infrared cameras, and audio recording devices in order to identify and record events that cannot be explained. These techniques, despite the fact that they are not without their detractors, give a level of impartiality that is necessary for scientific investigation and provide a method for measuring features of the paranormal.

In addition, developments in imaging technologies, such as thermal imaging and high-speed cameras, contribute to the process of gathering visual proof of paranormal activity. Researchers now have the ability to document anomalies that may occur beyond the visible spectrum or at rates that are incomprehensible to the human eye because of the tools that are available.

Interdisciplinary Methods and Strategies:

In light of the fact that paranormal occurrences are notoriously difficult to comprehend, there are researchers that argue for multidisciplinary approaches that incorporate the findings of their respective scientific fields.

For instance, the study of consciousness has emerged as a central focus in the process of comprehending psychic phenomena and altered states of awareness that are related with paranormal encounters.

It is essential to investigate the brain mechanisms that are responsible for paranormal perceptions and experiences, and neuroscience plays a significant part in this endeavor. Research that investigates the neurological correlates of altered states of consciousness, such as those that are brought about by meditation or by altered sensory inputs, contributes to our understanding of how the brain processes and interprets paranormal experiences.

A further point of interest is that the fields of psychology and cognitive science provide insightful perspectives on the role that perception, memory, and cognitive biases play in the formation of paranormal beliefs and experiences. When academics investigate the intersection of psychology and the paranormal, they are able to dissect the psychological processes that are at work in reported encounters with the supernatural.

One of the Functions of Citizen Science:

Over the past few years, the proliferation of citizen science programs has resulted in an expansion of the breadth of research into the paranormal. Amateur researchers and enthusiasts who are armed with easily available technology assist in the collecting and analysis of data, thereby establishing a decentralized method for the investigation of phenomena that are not adequately explained.

Projects that involve the collection of data from the general public, such as those that involve the sighting of unidentified flying objects or ghost hunting trips, offer researchers a plethora of material from a variety of locales and points of view. The sheer amount of reports makes it possible for patterns and trends to emerge, which provides useful insights for further scientific investigation. This is despite the fact that the veracity of such data is a cause for concern.

On the other hand, the participation of citizen scientists in paranormal research brings about a number of obstacles, including those concerning the quality of the data, the standardization of methodology, and the requirement for stringent oversight. Finding a way to retain scientific rigor while also capitalizing on the enthusiasm of amateur researchers is a difficulty that continues to be faced in this area of study.

Analysis of Psychophysiological Factors:

The investigation of the supernatural encompasses not only the subjective experiences and psychophysiological reactions of individuals, but also the exterior observations that are brought to light. In an effort to gain a better understanding of how the mind and body react to what others perceive to be supernatural occurrences, researchers have done studies that investigate the physiological changes that are connected with paranormal encounters.

In the course of paranormal investigations, studies on the physiological responses to fear and stress shed light on the complex relationship that exists between psychological causes and body reactions. The comprehension of these psychophysiological responses is a significant contributor to the investigation of the human experience of the supernatural in a more comprehensive manner.

The Disagreement and the Social Stigma:

The topic of paranormal research continues to be controversial within the larger scientific community, despite the progress that has been achieved in bringing scientific procedures to the investigation of the paranormal. When conventional scientists are confronted with the stigma that is connected with the study of the paranormal, they are frequently dissuaded from interacting with the subject matter. There are a number of factors that contribute to the reluctance to investigate paranormal experiences, including, but not limited to, concerns about career ramifications, skepticism from colleagues, and the possibility of compromising scientific credibility.

In addition, the absence of a consensus on established methodology and the replication of data is a barrier to the formation of a robust scientific foundation for the study of the paranormal. The intrinsic subjectivity of paranormal experiences, in conjunction with the difficulty of defining and measuring paranormal occurrences, contributes to the perpetuation of skepticism and skepticism within the scientific community.

What Is the Importance of Having an Open Mind?

In order to address the scientific investigation of the supernatural, it is necessary to strike a delicate balance between skepticism and open-minded investigative thinking. Researchers have a responsibility to acknowledge the limitations of the present scientific paradigms in terms of their ability to explain all elements of reality, while yet retaining a strict commitment to traditional scientific principles. Being open-minded means taking into account possibilities that are not conventional, being comfortable with ambiguity, and maintaining a receptive attitude toward the potential that phenomena that are currently classified as paranormal may one day find a place inside the recognized sphere of scientific understanding.

Steps that are essential to the process of legitimizing the scientific investigation of the unexplained include the promotion of interdisciplinary collaboration, the cultivation of research techniques that are open to scrutiny and can be replicated, and the establishment of a culture that is open to conversation about the supernatural. In order to make progress in our comprehension of the mysteries that lay outside ordinary experience, it is vital that the scientific community be willing to engage with these themes without completely ignoring them.

As we make our way through the intricate landscape of scientific investigation into the supernatural, we find ourselves at a crossroads where tradition and innovation, skepticism and open-mindedness all come together. Because of the inherent difficulties involved in the study of elusive and subjective phenomena, a strategy that is careful and diverse is required.

There are a number of possible options that might be pursued in order to broaden the scope of paranormal study. These include technological advancements, collaborations between scientific disciplines, and the participation of citizen scientists. Nevertheless, the scientific community continues to face a severe obstacle in the form of the stigma that is connected with the paranormal.

Researchers need to continue to refine methodology, be open to other points of view, and maintain vigilance in preserving the ideals of scientific inquiry in order to lay the groundwork for the scientific investigation of the paranormal. As we dive further into the mysteries that resist easy explanation, the scientific research of the paranormal stands as a tribute to the everlasting curiosity of humanity and the ever-evolving nature of our drive to grasp the elements that are beyond our comprehension.

1.2 Historical context and prevalent cultural perceptions

For the purpose of getting an understanding of the formation of collective consciousness and the development of societies, it is essential to have a profound comprehension of the historical context and the current cultural perceptions. There have been many different events, movements, and encounters that have played significant roles in shaping cultural conceptions throughout the course of history. In order to investigate the historical backdrop that has played a role in shaping societies, the purpose of this essay is to investigate the prevalent cultural conceptions that have formed as a result of this setting. We can gain a better understanding of the complex web of elements that contribute to the way civilizations perceive themselves and others if we look at significant historical periods and changes in society.

The Origins of Ancient Civilizations and the Foundations of Culture:

It is possible to trace the origins of present cultural perspectives all the way back to ancient civilizations, which were responsible for laying the foundation for societal conventions, values, and belief systems. Mesopotamia, Egypt, Greece, and Rome were among the important civilizations that played a significant role in the formation of the early foundations of human culture. The sophisticated systems of governance, religion, and social hierarchies that these cultures built laid the groundwork for subsequent generations to follow.

The Code of Hammurabi, which was discovered in ancient Mesopotamia, was a reflection of the legal and social conventions of the time. It offered insights into the organization of the society as well as the values that were upheld by its inhabitants. In a similar manner, the ancient Egyptian culture's notions of authority and spirituality were impacted by the pharaoh's divine status and the importance that ancient Egypt placed on the afterlife.

The contributions that the ancient Greek and Roman civilizations made to the fields of philosophy, politics, and the arts have had a significant and long-lasting effect on the culture of the Western world. During these time periods, important ideas such as democracy, individualism, and the pursuit of knowledge came into existence. These ideas laid the foundation for the cultural perspectives that would develop over the course of several centuries.

The Middle Ages: The Influence of Religion and the Feudal System:

During the Middle Ages, there was a tremendous shift in the cultural environment, which was characterized by the dominance of feudalism and the widespread influence of religion. A hierarchical framework consisting of lords, vassals, and serfs was the foundation upon which feudal civilizations were built. This structure contributed to diverse cultural notions of social order and class composition.

It was during this time period that religion, and more specifically Christianity, played a significant impact in the formation of cultural conceptions. Not only did the strength and authority of the Church have an effect on members' spiritual views, but it also had an effect on the norms and values of society. An example of this would be the Crusades, which were fueled by religious zeal and had a huge impact on the cultural contacts and perceptions that took place between the East and the West.

A cultural renaissance and an intellectual revolution: the Renaissance and the Enlightenment three centuries later

Europe experienced a cultural revival during the Renaissance period, which resulted in a resurgence of interest in the fields of art, literature, and humanism.

Some of the factors that contributed to a shift in cultural perceptions were the rediscovery of classical knowledge and the focus placed on individualism. In addition to promoting reason, scientific inquiry, and individual rights, the Enlightenment was a significant factor in the acceleration of this shift.

The invention of the printing press was a significant factor in the dissemination of ideas, the questioning of preexisting standards, and the formation of cultural conceptions. Thinkers such as Voltaire, Rousseau, and Locke were influential in the establishment of democratic ideals and human rights, and their writings posed a challenge to the authority that had been established in the past.

The Industrial Revolution and the Process of Modernization:

The Industrial Revolution was responsible for bringing about advances in technology, urbanization, and social transformations that had never been seen before. Cultural conceptions of work, family, and community saw significant shifts when civilizations migrated from rural economies to industrialized ones. These shifts occurred simultaneously.

The process of urbanization resulted in the development of various populations and the mingling of cultures in cities that were rapidly expanding. The transition from ways of life based on agriculture to ways of life based on industrialization in urban areas had a significant impact on the architecture of families and gender roles, which in turn altered cultural perceptions of conventional standards.

Conflicts, Social Movements, and the Globalization of the 20th Century:

There were two world wars that occurred during the 20th century, each of which had a significant impact on the geopolitical landscape and had far-reaching cultural ripples. The aftermath of these conflicts resulted in the Cold War, which resulted in the division of the world into ideological blocs and influenced cultural conceptions along political lines.

Cultural conceptions that were prevalent at the time regarding race, gender, and the power dynamics of colonial societies were challenged by movements such as the Civil Rights Movement, feminist groups, and decolonization attempts. Aiming to modify cultural attitudes toward diversity and tolerance, these social movements sought to eliminate structural disparities and bring about these changes.

Through the use of technology, commerce, and communication, the second half of the 20th century witnessed the acceleration of globalization, which connected cultures that were located in different countries.

This interconnectedness resulted in the sharing of ideas, the blending of cultures, and the development of a cultural landscape that is representative of the globalized world.

Perceptions of Contemporary Culture in the Present Day:

Throughout the 21st century, cultural conceptions continue to develop as a result of developments in technology, social movements, and shifts in geopolitical power. It is because of the advent of the digital age that the rapid sharing of information has been made possible, which has shaped global perceptions and influenced cultural narratives.

There have been debates and discussions that have been sparked by issues such as climate change, migration, and the rise of populism. These debates and discussions contribute to the process of cultural conceptions continuing to evolve. Because of the interconnected nature of the world, there is a greater need than ever before for cooperation and understanding amongst different cultures in order to address global concerns.

The historical context and the dominant cultural ideas are intimately connected, and they shape the way in which civilizations regard themselves and others. Each age has made a unique contribution to the intricate fabric that is human culture, beginning with the ancient civilizations that established the cultural foundations and continuing all the way up to the modern era of globalization. We are able to get a more profound comprehension of the dynamic nature of cultural perceptions and their ongoing evolution if we investigate the historical factors, societal shifts, and cultural movements that have played a role in shaping our viewpoints. As we traverse the difficulties of the present and look towards the future, it is becoming increasingly important to acknowledge the historical roots of cultural beliefs in order to cultivate a world that is more inclusive and linked.

1.3 Introduction to the concept of ghostly frequencies

Over the course of human history, the domain of the paranormal has been able to catch the imagination of people, resulting in stories of inexplicable happenings and otherworldly beings. When compared to the other phenomena that have captivated and baffled individuals, the idea of "ghostly frequencies" stands out as a subject that is both singular and mysterious. This essay intends to dig into the investigation of ghostly frequencies, with the goal of revealing the depths of this fascinating notion that connects the mysterious world of the supernatural with the scientific research of frequencies.

Let's define ghostly frequencies:

In the context of paranormal occurrences, particularly encounters with ghosts or spirits, the term "ghostly frequencies" refers to perceived signals, sounds, or vibrations that are connected with these phenomena.

Ghostly frequencies, on the other hand, are sometimes described as being subtle, elusive, and beyond the reach of ordinary human perception. This is in contrast to conventional frequencies, which can be easily verified through the use of scientific instruments.

Some people believe that these frequencies can present themselves in a variety of ways, such as electronic voice phenomena (EVP), sounds that are not typical, or even sensations that cannot be explained. When it comes to paranormal investigations, the investigation of ghostly frequencies interacts with the use of technologies like audio recording devices and electromagnetic field (EMF) meters. These techniques allow researchers to capture and evaluate potential spectral manifestations.

The Historical Context of Phenomena Related to the Paranormal:

There are profound historical origins to the belief in ghosts and other supernatural creatures, and these roots transcend both cultural boundaries and geographical limits. The stories of ghosts, apparitions, and other ethereal energy interacting with living people have been passed down from one civilization to the next throughout the course of human history. Throughout the history of human storytelling, the existence of ghosts has been a recurrent motif, appearing in everything from ancient folklore to holy scriptures.

The concept of ghostly frequencies is expressed in a variety of ways across cultures, including through rituals, spiritual activities, and attempts to speak with the departed. Many ancient civilizations, like the Greeks and the Egyptians, had the belief that there was an afterlife in which ghosts may exert their influence over the living. Spiritualism, which emerged in the 19th century, contributed to the widespread acceptance of the concept of communication with the afterlife through mediums, seances, and other acts that are considered to be paranormal.

Technological Developments and Investigations of the Paranormal:

The convergence of technology and the supernatural has resulted in the development of novel approaches to the investigation of ghostly audio frequencies. As technological breakthroughs in audio recording and electromagnetic detection techniques came into existence, investigators of the paranormal began to make use of scientific instruments in order to record and examine potential evidence of spectral activity.

The phenomenon known as Electronic Voice Phenomena (EVP), which involves the recording of voices or sounds that cannot be explained, has emerged as a central focus of research from the field of paranormal studies. The proponents of extra-sensory perception (EVP) contend that these strange sounds could be a representation of ghostly conversations or messages from beyond.

Furthermore, electromagnetic field meters are utilized by researchers in order to identify oscillations in electromagnetic fields. The researchers hypothesize that ghosts may alter these fields as a way of interaction.

Possible explanations for ghostly frequencies are as follows:

A number of hypotheses, spanning from the supernatural to the scientific, have been proposed in an effort to provide an explanation for the presence of ghostly frequencies. If spirits do exist, then one idea suggests that they may communicate with one another using frequencies that are outside the range of normal human hearing. This theory also suggests that these frequencies can be recorded and analyzed with the help of specialist equipment.

Skeptics frequently attribute the frequencies that they perceive to be ghostly to natural phenomena, such as electromagnetic interference, infrasound, or even psychological variables. This is done from a scientific point of view. For example, infrasound is made up of low-frequency vibrations that have the capacity to cause emotions of unease or fear, and they also have the potential to be misunderstood as ghostly phenomena.

Ghostly Frequencies and the Perceptions of Different Cultures:

The assumptions that people have concerning ghostly frequencies are significantly influenced by the cultural views that people have. The concept of the afterlife and the spiritual worlds is interpreted differently by various communities and religious traditions throughout the world. In many cases, an individual's cultural background, personal beliefs, and exposure to popular media all play a role in shaping how they view and interpret paranormal events.

At the same time as experiences with spirits are seen as a normal and unavoidable component of the human experience in some societies, they may be regarded with apprehension or skepticism in other societies. Another factor that contributes to cultural beliefs is the depiction of ghosts in works of literature, films, and television. These mediums play a significant role in determining how folks understand and interpret the mystery world of ghostly frequencies.

The Obstacles and the Skepticism:

There is still a significant amount of skepticism within the scientific community, despite the fact that there is a growing interest in ghostly frequencies and research of unusual phenomena. Many people believe that there is a lack of empirical evidence to support the existence of paranormal events, and that these experiences can be attributed to psychological causes, environmental conditions, or technical artifacts.

Additionally, skeptics underline the subjective character of personal experiences, drawing attention to the role that suggestion and anticipation play in the formation of beliefs of the supernatural. There is a great deal of skepticism surrounding the investigation of ghostly frequencies, which is further contributed to by the limitations of the technology that is now available and the difficulties of conducting controlled studies.

Considerations of Ethical Implications and Cultural Sensitivity:

Concerning cultural sensitivity and the potential influence on those who have encountered paranormal phenomena, the investigation of haunting frequencies involves ethical problems that need to be taken into account. The beliefs that people have on the afterlife and spiritual worlds are highly individualized and frequently connected to the traditions of their culture or religion. As a result, researchers and investigators are required to approach the topic with respect and cultural knowledge, acknowledging the variety of ideas and interpretations that exist.

Additionally, the publication of paranormal findings in the media has the potential to affect public attitudes and contribute to the perpetuation of sensationalism or stereotypes. For the purpose of ensuring that the investigation of ghostly frequencies is carried out with integrity and respect for those who share their experiences, ethical paranormal research places an emphasis on transparency, honesty, and responsible reporting.

I would like to conclude that the idea of phantom frequencies embodies a fascinating junction of science and the supernatural. The examination of these enigmatic frequencies has developed over time, thanks to developments in technology and investigations into the paranormal. These mysterious frequencies have their origins in historical beliefs and cultural customs. The study of ghostly frequencies continues to fascinate the human imagination and challenge our understanding of the borders between the natural and supernatural realms. This is true regardless of whether one approaches the topic with a sense of curiosity, skepticism, or a combination of the two. The conundrum of ghostly frequencies continues to be a trip of discovery, enticing us to investigate the enigmatic realms that may exist beyond the curtain of our everyday reality. This adventure of discovery is continuing as technology continues to progress and our collective knowledge continues to increase.

Chapter 2

The Quantum Connection: Where Science Meets the Supernatural

For a very long time, the junction of science and the supernatural has been a fascinating area of investigation as it has been the source of arguments, curiosity, and speculation. In the past few years, the subject of quantum physics has arisen as a focus point for the investigation of linkages between the scientific and the elements of reality that appear to be unexplainable. The purpose of this essay is to investigate the intricate relationship that exists between quantum physics and the supernatural, unveiling the fascinating hypotheses, debates, and consequences that emerge as a result of the convergence of these two realms.

The Basic Principles Constituting Quantum Physics:

A thorough investigation into the fundamentals of quantum physics is required in order to acquire an understanding of the quantum connection. Our knowledge of the underlying nature of matter and energy was fundamentally altered as a result of the development of quantum mechanics in the early 20th century. Max Planck, Albert Einstein, Niels Bohr, and Erwin Schrodinger were among the physicists that were instrumental in the development of quantum mechanics, which brought about a paradigm shift that posed a challenge to classical Newtonian physics.

The notion of quantization occupies a central position in quantum theory. This is the process by which particular physical attributes, such as energy levels, are quantized into discrete units, also known as quanta. Additionally, the concept of superposition argues that particles can exist in numerous states concurrently until they are observed, and the phenomena of entanglement suggests that particles can be instantaneously correlated regardless of the distance between them.

The Non-Locality of Quantum Entanglements and Entanglement:

Entanglement is one of the features of quantum physics that is the most difficult to understand. Because the states of two particles become connected when they become entangled, the measurement of the state of one particle can instantly determine the state of the other particle, regardless of the distance that separates them. This occurrence presents a challenge to the traditional ideas of causality and location, which ultimately led to the development of the idea of non-locality.

There have been some theorists and researchers that have made comparisons between quantum entanglement and certain things that are considered to be supernatural or metaphysical. The idea of interconnectedness in spiritual or mystical traditions, in which everything in the cosmos is viewed as interconnected at a fundamental level, has been compared to the instantaneous connection that exists between particles that are entangled with one another.

The Observer Effect and Consciousness:

The quantum connection is presented with an additional layer when one considers the role that consciousness plays in quantum physics. The observer effect is a key idea in quantum mechanics that proposes that the act of observing or measuring quantum phenomena has an effect on the outcomes of those phenomena. Through the simple act of seeing a particle, its wave function collapses, and the state of the particle is determined.

As a result of this connection between observation and the behavior of quantum particles, speculation has arisen over the part that consciousness plays in the manner in which reality appears. Parallels are drawn between the quantum connection and metaphysical conceptions that postulate a relationship between mind and matter. Some proponents of the quantum connection think that awareness plays a vital role in the manifestation of physical reality.

Theories of Quantum Superposition and the Multiverse

The idea that particles can exist in numerous states concurrently until they are observed is a basic tenet of quantum physics. This idea is known as the concept of superposition. The nature of reality and the potential of parallel universes have both been brought up in conversations that have been spurred by this topic.

According to multiverse theories, there are numerous universes that live with one another, each of which has its own unique set of physical constants and environment. The act of observing or measuring anything could potentially result in the branching of universes, each of which represents a possible outcome, according to certain interpretations of quantum physics. The concept of parallel realities has exciting implications for comprehending phenomena that are sometimes linked with the supernatural, such as memories of the past or the ability to predict the future.

The Quantum Tunneling Process and Other Extraordinary Occurrences:

The phenomenon of quantum tunneling, in which particles are able to pass through energy barriers that are considered impenetrable by classical physics, has been cited in order to provide an explanation for a number of paranormal occurrences.

Past the process of tunneling, particles are able to "jump" past energy barriers without having to travel through the space in between. This type of process contradicts traditional ideas about the limitations of physical space.

In recent years, there has been a growing body of speculation concerning the potential application of quantum tunneling to phenomena such as telepathy, telekinesis, and other supposed psychic powers. The investigation of quantum tunneling in the context of paranormal experiences is an example of an attempt to bridge the gap between scientific understanding and the unexplained, despite the fact that the scientific community continues to maintain its skepticism.

Introducing the Holographic Universe and the Concept of Reality as Information:

Our three-dimensional reality is a projection of information that is encoded on a two-dimensional surface, according to the holographic universe hypothesis, which posits that this would be the case. Through the application of this idea, parallels are drawn between the structure of a hologram and the nature of the reality that we perceive.

The holographic universe concept is being investigated by researchers, and their findings suggest that reality may be more changeable than was previously believed. It is possible to contemplate the potential that consciousness, intention, or other influences could change the holographic information that manifests as our experienced reality if our perspective of reality is comparable to a holographic projection. This opens the door to the possibility that our perception of reality is similar to a holographic projection.

Quantum spirituality and mystical experiences

Quantum spirituality is a notion that emerged as a result of the convergence of quantum physics and spirituality. In this concept, the fundamentals of quantum mechanics are incorporated into frameworks that are either spiritual or metaphysical. Quantum physics, according to the arguments of some proponents, offers a scientific foundation for comprehending spiritual experiences, awareness, and the linked nature of everything.

There is a common practice of citing mystical experiences in conversations on the quantum connection. These experiences include those that individuals describe having while in altered states of consciousness or while engaging in intense meditation. The disintegration of barriers between the self and the world, as observed by mystics, finds resonance with the connectivity that is implied by quantum entanglement and non-locality.

Challenges, criticisms, and ethical considerations

The investigation of the quantum connection, despite the fact that it opens up exciting possibilities, is not without its problems and critics. A number of individuals within the scientific community are of the opinion that attempts to draw a connection between quantum events and the supernatural sometimes entail misinterpretations or extrapolations that go beyond the recognized rules of quantum physics.

It is important to take into consideration ethical issues because there is a possibility that scientific notions could be misunderstood or misrepresented when applied to the supernatural. In order to maintain the rigor and integrity of scientific inquiry while also investigating speculative notions, scientists and researchers need to navigate the delicate balance that exists between the two perspectives. It is also important to take into account ethical considerations when it comes to the manner in which these concepts are communicated to the general public, as misunderstandings can lead to the spread of false information and keep pseudoscientific views alive.

Prospective Courses of Action and Their Implications:

The investigation of the quantum connection continues to be a dynamic and ever-evolving topic, with research and theoretical advancements undergoing continuous improvement. It is possible that new discoveries will emerge that further highlight the linkages between quantum physics and the supernatural as technology continues to develop and our understanding of quantum phenomena continues to increase.

In addition to the worlds of physics and metaphysics, the quantum connection has consequences that transcend beyond those two fields. In the event that we get a more profound comprehension of the dynamic relationship that exists between science and the supernatural, our ideas on consciousness, reality, and the essence of existence may undergo a transformation. The purpose of this interdisciplinary investigation is to encourage collaboration between scientists, philosophers, theologians, and intellectuals from a variety of fields in order to solve the mysteries that are located at the intersection of the known and the unknown.

A frontier of study that captivates the imagination and challenges our perception of reality is the endeavor to unravel the quantum connection, which will take place at the intersection of science and the supernatural. The convergence of science and the supernatural encourages us to reevaluate the limits of our knowledge, because it encompasses everything from the fundamentals of quantum mechanics to the investigation of consciousness and the mysteries of the universe.

In order to successfully navigate this complicated landscape, it is essential that we approach the topic with a combination of scientific rigor, open-minded research, and ethical considerations taken into account. We are encouraged to ponder the nature of reality, the function of consciousness, and the possibility of realms that are beyond our immediate perception as a result of the quantum connection.

The voyage itself is a testament to the human spirit of inquiry, curiosity, and the unrelenting desire of understanding the mysteries that surround us. Whether one considers the quantum connection as a bridge between the scientific and the supernatural or as a speculative exploration, the journey itself is a testament to the human spirit.

2.1 Exploring quantum physics and its potential links to the paranormal

For a very long time, quantum physics, which is the subfield of physics that examines the behavior of particles on the lowest sizes, has been a source of both intrigue and mystery. There has been a growing interest in investigating the possibility of connections between quantum physics and supernatural occurrences throughout the course of the past few years. The purpose of this essay is to investigate the intriguing similarities that certain theorists and researchers propose between the laws of quantum physics and unexplained occurrences that are frequently connected with the paranormal.

Non-Locality and Quantum Entanglement: Considerations

When it comes to quantum physics, entanglement is one of the fundamental ideas that has inspired conversations about the possible connections between quantum mechanics and the supernatural. Entanglement takes place when two particles become linked in such a way that the state of one particle is directly tied to the state of the other particle, regardless of the distance that separates them. Because of this instantaneous connectivity, our traditional notion of causality and locality is being called into question.

On the other hand, there are theorists who believe that the idea of non-locality, which is inherent in quantum entanglement, could provide a framework for comprehending the occurrence of paranormal phenomena. A comparison has been made between the interconnectedness that is frequently expressed in spiritual or metaphysical traditions and the concept that particles can be connected beyond the confines of space and time. As a result of this relationship, discussion has been fanned over the possibility that certain paranormal experiences involve a sort of non-local interaction that goes beyond the confines of traditional physical space.

The Observer Effect and the Formation of Consciousness:

The observer effect is just another facet of quantum physics that has sparked interest in the domain of the supernatural. In accordance with this principle, the act of observing or measuring anything has an effect on the results of quantum events. Through the simple act of seeing a particle, its wave function collapses, and the state of the particle is determined.

One school of thought contends that consciousness itself plays a significant part in the formation of reality. They do this by drawing parallels between the observer effect and the function that awareness plays in the occurrence of paranormal events. From this point of view, it is possible that the mind of the viewer may interact with the quantum realm in ways that lead to phenomena that cannot be explained, such as telepathy, telekinesis, or precognition.

Realities that are parallel to one another and quantum superposition:

Within the realm of quantum mechanics, the concept of superposition asserts that particles are capable of existing in several states simultaneously until they are seen. Discussions have arisen as a result of this idea regarding the potential of parallel realities or numerous universes coexisting despite their differences. In certain interpretations of quantum physics, it is proposed that the act of observing or measuring something might result in the branching of universes, with each universe representing a distinct outcome.

This concept, when considered in the context of the paranormal, raises questions regarding the possibility that certain experiences, such as precognition or déjà vu, could represent glimpses into parallel universes. For the purpose of comprehending occurrences that defy traditional explanations, the idea that our sense of reality is not static but rather exists in a superposition of possibilities offers up exciting possibilities.

Psychic Phenomena and Quantum Tunneling:

When attempting to explain certain psychic occurrences, the concept of quantum tunneling has been raised. This refers to the phenomenon in which particles are able to pass through energy barriers that classical physics considers to be impenetrable. past the process of tunneling, particles are able to "jump" past energy barriers without having to actually go through the space in between, which challenges the conventional understanding of physical boundaries.

Quantum tunneling is a theory that has been proposed by a number of theorists as a potential mechanism at the root of phenomena such as telepathy and clairvoyance. Even if these concepts are still considered to be speculative, the fact that an attempt has been made to bridge the gap between quantum physics and psychic experiences demonstrates a desire to investigate alternative paths in the pursuit of comprehension.

The Holographic Universe and Information:

According to the holographic universe hypothesis, the three-dimensional reality that we experience is believed to be a projection of information that is encoded on a surface that is only two-dimensional. Through the application of this idea, parallels are drawn between the structure of a hologram and the nature of the reality that we perceive.

The holographic universe hypothesis, when considered in the context of the paranormal, raises questions regarding the malleability of reality and the role that consciousness plays in molding the information that manifests as the world that we experience. In the event that reality is comparable to a holographic projection, the influence of the mind on the information that is encoded becomes an essential factor to take into account when attempting to comprehend paranormal occurrences.

The Obstacles and the Skepticism:

Although the investigation of possible connections between quantum physics and the supernatural is fascinating, it is not without its difficulties and skepticism despite the fact that it is engaging. In the process of attempting to establish a connection between quantum phenomena and paranormal experiences, many scientists say that these attempts frequently entail erroneous interpretations or speculative extrapolations that go beyond the known laws of quantum physics.

In order to validate any hypothesized linkages between quantum physics and the paranormal, skeptics emphasize the importance of being able to provide empirical evidence and conducting controlled tests. The lack of agreement among members of the scientific community over how quantum phenomena should be interpreted is one factor that contributes to the skepticism that surrounds these explorations.

Considerations of an Ethical Nature:

Ethical questions are raised when one investigates the possibility of linkages between quantum physics and the supernatural, particularly with regard to the manner in which these concepts are communicated to the general public. It is possible for the media to contribute to the propagation of pseudoscientific views and misinformation by misinterpreting and sensationalizing certain events.

Between the exploration of speculative ideas and the preservation of the integrity of scientific inquiry, researchers and theorists are required to navigate the ethical balance that exists between the two.

It is essential to engage in responsible communication regarding the possible connections between quantum physics and the paranormal in order to prevent the general public from being misled and to encourage the development of a nuanced knowledge of the complicated issues that are at play.

Prospective Courses of Action and Their Implications:

The investigation of quantum physics and the possible connections it may have with the supernatural continues to be a vibrant and progressive subject of study. It is possible that the inexplicable intersections between quantum physics and unexplained events can be cast some light on by ongoing research, technological improvements, and collaboration across disciplines.

In addition to the domains of physics and the supernatural, these investigations have consequences that go beyond those two fields. A more in-depth comprehension of the dynamic relationship that exists between quantum principles and paranormal experiences has the potential to transform our beliefs on consciousness, reality, and the fundamental nature of existence. It encourages us to reevaluate the limits of our knowledge and investigate new lines of research that can help us bridge the gap between what we know and what we don't know.

The investigation of possible connections between quantum physics and the supernatural constitutes an intriguing new avenue of research. The crossovers between quantum mechanics and unexplained events give up new avenues for comprehending the mysteries that are all around us. These intersections include the notions of entanglement and non-locality, as well as the observer effect and the holographic nature of reality.

It is a reflection of the intrinsic curiosity of the human intellect that people are eager to examine uncommon ideas, despite the fact that skepticism and problems continue today. The path of exploration itself provides vital insights into the nature of reality and the quest for understanding the unexplained, regardless of whether these potential relationships are subsequently proven by empirical evidence or remain for the time being hypothetical. The research of quantum physics and its potential linkages to the paranormal stands as a tribute to the everlasting human spirit of inquiry and fascination with the strange. This is especially true in light of the fact that science and the paranormal continue to dance on the edge of our comprehension.

2.2 Quantum entanglement and its implications for spectral interactions

Since the early formulation of quantum physics in the 20th century, the phenomenon of quantum entanglement, which is a phenomenon that counteracts classical intuitions, has been a fundamental component of quantum physics. In this essay, the complexities of quantum entanglement are investigated, and the potential implications that it may have for spectral interactions are investigated as well. Spectral interactions are phenomena that are frequently connected with the supernatural or the paranormal. In the process of navigating the complexity of quantum entanglement, we are attempting to understand its mysteries and contemplate the ways in which it may throw light on the mysterious world of spectral occurrences during our exploration.

Comprehending the Concept of Quantum Entanglement:

Quantum entanglement is a phenomenon that occurs in quantum mechanics and occurs when two or more particles become correlated to the extent that the state of one particle is directly related to the state of another particle, regardless of the physical distance that separates them. In the case of entangled particles, the measurement of the state of one particle can instantly determine the state of the other particle, even if the two particles are separated by light-years between them.

Both the traditional concepts of locality and causality are called into question by this phenomenon. The famed scientist Albert Einstein once characterized entanglement as "spooky action at a distance" because it appeared to contradict the principle of locality, which states that information or influence cannot move faster than the speed of light.

In the process of creating two or more particles or interacting with them in such a way that their quantum states become intertwined, a phenomenon known as quantum entanglement takes place. The entanglement between the particles continues to exist regardless of the distance that separates them spatially, which results in correlations that appear to be in contradiction with our traditional knowledge of the physical universe.

Relationships between Spectral Interactions and Entanglement:

The perception or manifestation of creatures, energies, or phenomena that exist beyond the purview of typical human experiences is what is meant by the term "spectral interactions." Spectral interactions are usually connected with paranormal or supernatural events. These encounters are frequently described in terms of apparitions, ghostly presences, or sensory impressions that cannot be explained beyond a reasonable doubt.

The instantaneous correlation of quantum states presents a potential relationship between quantum entanglement and spectral interactions. This correlation can occur even at substantial distances between the two phenomena. There are some theorists who believe that the entanglement of particles might extend beyond the world of the microscopic and might have ramifications for macroscopic events, such as those that are observed in spectral interactions.

The theory is hypothetical, and there is no empirical data to explicitly suggest a connection between quantum entanglement and spectral events at the present time. The investigation of this theoretical relationship, on the other hand, offers a framework for contemplating the strange and frequently evasive character of spectral interactions.

Non-Locality and Quantum Spookiness:

It is fascinating to consider the implications that the non-locality that is inherent in quantum entanglement, in which particles continue to be instantaneously correlated regardless of distance, has for the idea of quantum spookiness. If particles are able to get entangled in a way that remains consistent across enormous distances, then it is possible that this phenomena may extend to the macroscopic environment and influence the interactions of spectral waves.

Quantum spookiness is a term that is frequently used to describe the mysterious parts of quantum physics; nonetheless, it is vital to approach this topic with a mix of curiosity and scientific rigor in order to fully comprehend it. It is necessary to give serious thought to both the scientific concepts that are already in place and the empirical evidence that is available in order to investigate the possibility of linkages between non-local quantum phenomena and spectral interactions.

Quantum States and Spectral Manifestations

Questions regarding the nature of reality and the potential influence of quantum processes on human perceptual experiences are brought up as a result of the entanglement of quantum states. Are the spectral manifestations that have been recorded in a variety of cultural and historical contexts possible to be the result of entangled quantum states producing them?

It has been suggested by a number of theorists that the entanglement of particles could potentially have an effect on the perceptual experiences of individuals, which would then result in occurrences that are typically linked with the supernatural. This theoretical theory indicates that the correlations that are generated at the quantum level could extend to macroscopic sizes, influencing the interactions that take place between the quantum world and our perceptual reality.

The Observer Effect and Spectral Experiences:

The observer effect is another essential notion in quantum physics. It proposes that the act of observing or measuring something has an effect on the outcome of quantum events. In the course of conversations concerning awareness and the possible part it plays in the formation of reality, this principle was brought up.

Within the framework of spectral interactions, the observer effect gives rise to a number of intriguing concerns concerning the impact that consciousness has on the manner in which paranormal occurrences present themselves. Considering that the act of observation has the ability to affect quantum states, it is possible that it might also play a part in the formation of individuals' perceptions and experiences while they are in the presence of spectral phenomena.

The relationship between parallel realities and quantum superposition

Parallel realities are influenced by the superposition principle, which asserts that particles can exist in numerous states concurrently until they are seen. This principle has ramifications for the concept of parallel realities. The act of observing or measuring something can, according to some interpretations of quantum physics, result in the branching of universes, each of which represents a different outcome.

The concept of parallel realities, when applied to the context of spectral interactions, paves the way for the possibility of comprehending the coexistence of many perceptual experiences. When seen through the perspective of parallel worlds that emerge from the rules of quantum superposition, reports of individuals who witnessed the same paranormal event but described it in different ways could be interpreted very differently.

Obstacles and Negative Opinions:

The investigation of possible connections between quantum entanglement and spectral interactions is a fascinating endeavor; nonetheless, it is not devoid of difficulties and skepticism. Several members of the scientific community have emphasized the importance of conducting controlled tests and gathering empirical evidence in order to validate any claimed linkages between quantum events and personal experiences of the paranormal.

It is the contention of skeptics that the application of quantum principles to macroscopic phenomena, particularly those connected with the paranormal, is speculative extrapolations that go beyond the accepted boundaries of quantum physics. In addition to the difficulties associated with drawing obvious connections between quantum entanglement and spectral interactions, the complexities of human perception, cognitive biases, and cultural influences are other factors that contribute to these difficult hurdles.

Considerations of an Ethical Nature:

The search of linkages between quantum entanglement and spectral interactions presents ethical problems, particularly with regard to the manner in which these concepts are communicated to the general public during the experiment. The sharing of speculative theories in a responsible manner is absolutely necessary in order to prevent contributing to the spread of false information or pseudoscientific views.

The examination of these potential relationships needs to be approached with honesty by researchers and theorists. They should acknowledge the speculative nature of the concepts and place an emphasis on the significance of empirical evidence in scientific inquiry. As a result of the fact that misunderstandings can contribute to the persistence of views that are not supported by evidence, ethical problems also extend to the manner in which these ideas are portrayed in the media.

The examination of putative linkages between quantum entanglement and spectral interactions presents an intriguing convergence of quantum physics and the paranormal. The observer effect, non-locality, and the entanglement of quantum states all pose intriguing concerns about the nature of reality and the possible linkages between the tiny world of quantum mechanics and the macroscopic world of perceptual experiences. These questions are raised in relation to the entanglement of quantum states.

Despite the fact that the theoretical investigation of these relationships is based on speculation, it serves as a demonstration of the human spirit of inquiry and the constant search to comprehend the mysteries that are all around us. The exploration of quantum entanglement and its potential implications for spectral interactions invites us to contemplate the unknown and reconsider the boundaries of our understanding of both the quantum and the spectral realms. This investigation comes at a time when science and the paranormal continue to dance at the edges of our comprehension.

2.3 Theoretical frameworks connecting quantum mechanics to ghostly phenomena

Throughout the course of human history, the mysterious realm of ghostly phenomena has captivated the imagination of humans, which has resulted in the development of a wide range of cultural beliefs, folklore, and instances of paranormal experiences. In recent years, there has been an increasing interest in studying theoretical connections between quantum mechanics, the fundamental theory that governs the behavior of matter and energy at the lowest scales, and the unexplained events connected with ghosts. This interest has been fueled by the fact that quantum mechanics is now being studied. This essay dives into theoretical frameworks that attempt to build connections between quantum mechanics and ghostly experiences.

It also investigates the possibilities that come about as a result of the intersection between the secrets of the quantum world and the mysteries of the paranormal.

Non-Locality and Quantum Entanglement: Considerations

The phenomenon of quantum entanglement, which occurs when particles become correlated in such a way that the state of one particle is directly related to the state of another particle, regardless of the distance between them, has been the focal point of theoretical discussions regarding its possible connection to ghostly phenomena.

Quantum entanglement, according to the postulations of certain theorists, might potentially extend beyond the microscopic scale and exert an influence on macroscopic events that are connected with ghosts. The fact that quantum states can instantly correlate with one another, even when they are separated by large distances, raises questions regarding the nature of interactions that are not local. It is possible that the entanglement of particles could offer a theoretical framework that has the potential to provide an understanding of how entities or energy connected with ghosts might interact with the physical world in a manner that is not local.

The examination of quantum entanglement as a theoretical basis for ghostly occurrences gives a different viewpoint on the nature of interactions that may occur outside our conventional knowledge. Despite the fact that the theory is hypothetical and does not have any empirical backing, it is nevertheless interesting to have this new perspective.

The Observer Effect and the Concept of Consciousness:

The observer effect is a key idea in quantum mechanics that proposes that the act of observing or measuring something has an effect on the outcome of quantum events. Taking into consideration the implications of this concept in the context of ghostly occurrences, particularly in regard to the function of consciousness, offers some fascinating possibilities.

It has been suggested by a number of theorists that awareness plays a significant part in the formation of reality. These theorists have drawn parallels between the observer effect and the probable influence of human consciousness on the apparition of ghosts. The concept suggests that the presence of an observer, whether it be a conscious individual or a recording equipment, may have an effect on the manner in which ghostly occurrences are viewed or how they interact with the physical world.

This theoretical framework encourages thought about the nature of consciousness and the possible connection that it may have with the manifestation of paranormal experiences.

The fact that it raises issues regarding the observer effect and how it might be connected to the experiences of people who claim to have had meetings with ghosts, as well as whether or not the consciousness of the observer has an effect on the characteristics of the events that are being witnessed.

Realities that are parallel to one another and quantum superposition:
In quantum physics, the concept of superposition, which asserts that particles can exist in several states simultaneously until they are seen, is a fundamental principle. This concept is expanded upon by some theorists, who propose linkages between quantum superposition and the presence of parallel realities. Parallel realities are a type of reality in which alternative outcomes occur in distinct branches of the universe.

In the context of spectral phenomena, the theoretical framework of quantum superposition and parallel worlds provides the potential that ghosts could exist in a state of superposition, appearing in several ways or states concurrently. This is a possibility that is introduced by the framework. It is possible that this concept could provide an explanation for the various and frequently inconsistent nature of the ghostly encounters that have been reported, in which different viewers may see ghosts in different ways.

In addition, the idea of parallel worlds brings up problems concerning the nature of time and space in respect to spectral phenomena. Our conventional understanding of the time and spatial limits associated with paranormal encounters is called into question by the possibility that ghosts live in superposition across several universes.

Tunneling through quantum mechanics and traveling across dimensions:
Quantum tunneling, a phenomenon in which particles are able to pass through energy barriers that classical physics considers to be impenetrable, has been invoked in order to investigate theoretical frameworks that connect quantum mechanics to interdimensional travel. This is a concept that is consistent with certain interpretations of ghostly phenomena.

From a theoretical standpoint, it has been suggested that entities or energies linked with ghosts could potentially exploit quantum tunneling in order to travel through dimensions or worlds that are beyond our normal perception. Based on this theory, it is possible that the apparitions or manifestations that appear to be ghosts could be the consequence of interdimensional travel that is made possible by the laws of quantum tunneling.

A multidimensional perspective that challenges conventional concepts of space and reality is introduced through the investigation of quantum tunneling as a theoretical basis for interdimensional transit in the setting of ghostly experiences. This investigation is speculative, but it presents a multidimensional perspective.

When it comes to information and quantum holography:

Another theoretical framework for describing ghostly events within the realm of quantum physics is introduced by the holographic universe hypothesis. This theory proposes that our three-dimensional reality is a projection of information encoded on a surface that is only two-dimensional.

The theory of quantum holography postulates that information concerning spectral beings or experiences might be encoded on a quantum level, which would have an effect on the manner in which these phenomena emerge in our perception of reality. There is a connection between this framework and the concept that the nature of ghostly interactions may include the manipulation of holographic information on a quantum scale.

The investigation of quantum holography as a theoretical foundation for comprehending spectral phenomena offers up the possibility of reinventing the nature of information and consciousness, as well as the potential linkages that exist between the quantum world and the supernatural.

The Obstacles and the Skepticism:

It is crucial to acknowledge the obstacles and skepticism that exist within the scientific community, despite the fact that these theoretical frameworks offer intriguing insights on the potential linkages between quantum mechanics and ghostly events. Many researchers in the field of science contend that the application of quantum principles to macroscopic phenomena, particularly those that are associated with the supernatural, constitutes speculative extrapolations that go beyond the recognized boundaries of quantum physics.

For the purpose of validating any hypothesized linkages between quantum events and ghostly encounters, skeptics emphasize the significance of empirical evidence and controlled experiments. In addition to the difficulties associated with drawing unambiguous connections between quantum mechanics and ghostly events, the complexities of human perception, cognitive biases, and cultural influences all contribute to the difficulties this presents.

Considerations of an Ethical Nature:

The investigation of theoretical frameworks that link quantum physics to spectral phenomena presents ethical concerns, particularly with regard to the manner in which these concepts are communicated to the general public. The sharing of speculative theories in a responsible manner is absolutely necessary in order to prevent contributing to the spread of false information or pseudoscientific views.

The examination of these potential relationships needs to be approached with honesty by researchers and theorists. They should acknowledge the speculative nature of the concepts and place an emphasis on the significance of empirical evidence in scientific inquiry. As a result of the fact that misunderstandings can contribute to the persistence of views that are not supported by evidence, ethical problems also extend to the manner in which these ideas are portrayed in the media.

The theoretical frameworks that provide a connection between quantum mechanics and ghostly occurrences provide innovative views on the mysteries that are all around us. These frameworks present innovative ways of pondering the nature of ghostly interactions within the setting of quantum physics. Ranging from quantum entanglement and the observer effect to quantum superposition and holography, these frameworks all have their own unique characteristics.

The investigation of these notions, despite the fact that they are still speculative and do not have any empirical backing, stands as a tribute to the everlasting human spirit of inquiry and the constant search to understand the unknown. The theoretical frameworks that relate quantum mechanics to ghostly events urge us to imagine new possibilities and to reevaluate the limitations of our understanding of both the quantum and the spectral realms. This is necessary since science and the paranormal continue to become intertwined in the fabric of human curiosity.

Chapter 3

The Energy of Apparitions: Ectoplasmic Manifestations

From the beginning of time, the human imagination has been captivated by the investigation of supernatural occurrences, with apparitions and ghostly encounters serving as major elements in cultural narratives all throughout the world. There is a phenomena known as ectoplasm, which is a mystery substance that is said to radiate from or be linked with apparitions. This phenomenon is one compelling component of these encounters. The purpose of this essay is to investigate the historical origins, scientific investigations, and cultural perspectives that surround ectoplasmic occurrences. The goal is to solve the mystery of this ethereal material and its connection to the world of the supernatural.

Ectoplasm's Historical beginnings and origins:

The concept of ectoplasm has strong historical roots, extending back to the late 19th and early 20th centuries, when spiritualism was at its height of popularity. Through the use of mediums, the religious and philosophical movement known as spiritualism attempted to establish communication with the spirits of those who had passed away earlier. Mediums claimed to be able to manufacture a substance that acted as a channel for spirit manifestations during séances, which led to the emergence of ectoplasm as a major characteristic of these events.

One of the oldest references to ectoplasm may be traced back to the work of Charles Richet, a French biologist and Nobel laureate. Richet used the term to describe a fluid that he felt was secreted by certain mediums while they were in a trance state. In the context of spiritualist rituals, Richet's observations cleared the ground for future investigation into the phenomenon of ectoplasm.

Identification of Ectoplasm's Characteristics:

Ectoplasm is a substance that is distinguished from other types of matter by its distinctive properties, which are stated in the previous sentence. Ectoplasm is described as a semi-transparent or milky-white fluid that emits from the body of a medium while they are in a trance, according to accounts from spiritualist circles and events that take place during séances. It is frequently shown as having an otherworldly and ethereal appearance, and it can sometimes take on forms such as tendrils, mist, or even solid objects.

People who claimed to be mediums asserted that ectoplasm acted as a medium via which spirits may materialize and speak with living people. Light was claimed to be sensitive to the substance, and it was said that if it was quickly exposed to light, it may either disappear or retract. In the course of the séances, witnesses have reported witnessing apparitions or spirit forms emerging from the ectoplasmic mist.

Spiritualism and the Practice of Mediumship:

There was a boom in the number of séances and the practice of mediumship during the period of spiritualism, which reached its zenith in the latter half of the 19th century and the early 20th century. Individuals who are believed to have the ability to connect with the spirit realm were known as mediums, and they played a significant role in these gatherings. Mediums asserted that they were able to assist connection with spirits that had passed away through the formation of ectoplasm, which led to the emergence of ectoplasmic manifestations as a central component of séances.

Several notable mediums, including Eva C. and Kluski, have garnered attention due to the fact that they are rumored to be capable of producing ectoplasmic manifestations. A significant amount of visual mystery was added to the spiritualist movement by the use of photographs taken during séances. These photographs frequently featured mediums surrounded by the enigmatic material.

Skepticism and the Investigations of the Scientific Community:

At the same time that ectoplasmic occurrences caught the attention of the general public, they also became the focus of scientific investigation. A number of individuals, including researchers and skeptics, endeavored to explore the nature of ectoplasm in order to ascertain whether or not it was founded on empirical reality or whether it was the result of trickery.

Harry Price, a British psychical researcher, was a significant player in this examination. He was responsible for conducting a large number of studies to investigate the veracity of ectoplasmic occurrences. Price's study, on the other hand, frequently led to the exposure of fraudulent practices among mediums, which in turn led to an increase in suspicion regarding the veracity of ectoplasmic appearances.

Skeptics believed that many cases of ectoplasmic occurrences were the result of deliberate trickery, with mediums utilizing various materials, such as cheesecloth, muslin, or even regurgitated substances, to generate the appearance of ectoplasm. This was one of the arguments that was made by skeptics. The low-light circumstances that are present during séances, according to critics, provide an excellent atmosphere for the perpetration of such deceptions.

Ectoplasm from a Contemporary Perspective:

Even though the popularity of spiritualism began to decline in the middle of the 20th century, the idea of ectoplasm continued to be prevalent in popular culture. This was especially true in depictions of ghosts and other supernatural events that were found in stories, movies, and television shows. The concept of ectoplasm as a material substance that is related with spectral occurrences became deeply embedded in the popular imagination.

When it comes to modern investigations into the paranormal, the term "ectoplasm" is frequently used in a more general sense to refer to unusual substances or energy readings that are obtained during ghost hunting. Infrared cameras and electromagnetic field (EMF) meters are examples of the modern technology that is utilized in the process of identifying and documenting the presence of probable ectoplasmic activity.

The scientific community, on the other hand, continues to maintain a widespread skepticism regarding the reality of ectoplasm as a supernatural or paranormal substance. Those who are opposed to ectoplasmic appearances believe that the credibility of these manifestations is undermined by the absence of empirical proof and the prevalence of deception in historical examples.

Perspectives on Culture and the Influence of Popular Media:

Because of the lasting impression that ectoplasmic appearances have left on popular culture, the manner in which ghosts and spirits are portrayed in literature, cinema, and television has been irrevocably altered. One of the most recognizable aspects of the spooky genre is the concept of ectoplasm, which is portrayed as a mysterious substance that connects the material and spiritual realms.

In works of literature, ectoplasmic manifestations are frequently incorporated into ghost stories, which contributes to the atmospheric and frightening elements of narratives that are associated with the paranormal. In the world of film, the classic sights of ectoplasmic mist wrapping ghostly figures have become synonymous with the horror genre and the supernatural.

Television shows that investigate paranormal occurrences, such as those that are centered on ghost hunting or investigations into haunted locales, sometimes make mention of ectoplasm as a possible indicator of spiritual activity. The degree to which these images conform to scientific rigor, on the other hand, varies greatly, and they frequently combine parts of amusement with elements of the supernatural.

Quantum perspectives on ghostly energy:

Some theorists and researchers have investigated various frameworks to explain ghostly events, including the potential of quantum interactions, as scientific understanding has progressed. For example, quantum interactions have been considered. It has been suggested that quantum physics, with its principles of non-locality, entanglement, and the observer effect, could be utilized in order to investigate the potential energy dynamics that are linked with visual phenomena.

It has been suggested by proponents of quantum perspectives on ghostly energy that the entanglement of particles or the influence of consciousness on quantum states may provide insights into the manner in which ghosts interact with the physical world. In these speculative theories, it is proposed that quantum phenomena could offer a scientific foundation for comprehending the mysterious energy that is linked with apparitions.

Despite the fact that these quantum perspectives are still considered to be speculative and are not commonly recognized within the scientific mainstream, they are indicative of a continued curiosity regarding the possible connections that exist between the quantum domain and paranormal experiences.

The consideration of ethical issues and the conduct of responsible investigations:

Given the nature of paranormal investigations, the research of ectoplasmic manifestations and ghostly events poses ethical concerns that need to be taken into consideration. Researchers and investigators who are responsible for their work must traverse the difficult balance that exists between engaging in serious inquiry, providing entertainment, and the possibility of sensationalism.

Throughout history, there have been cases of fraud and deception surrounding ectoplasmic phenomena. These occurrences show the significance of maintaining strict standards in the field of paranormal study. Ethical considerations extend to the manner in which these phenomena are communicated to the general public, with an emphasis on transparency, skepticism, and the acceptance of uncertainty in the face of the unexplained.

One of the most fascinating aspects of the interaction between the paranormal and human awareness is the mystery surrounding ectoplasmic phenomena, which continues to be a mystery. The idea of ectoplasm continues to pique people's interest and provoke controversy, not only because of its historical origins in spiritualism but also because of scientific investigations, cultural depictions, and theoretical quantum perspectives.

Despite the fact that the scientific world continues to maintain a general skepticism regarding the existence of ectoplasm as a paranormal substance, the everlasting interest with this ethereal element is a testament to the everlasting appeal of the unknown. We are invited to explore the strange and to reevaluate the boundaries of our understanding of the energies that may connect the living and the spectral as we navigate the worlds of the supernatural and the scientific. This is because the exploration of ectoplasmic phenomena asks us to do so.

3.1 Examining the potential energy sources behind ghostly apparitions

As a result of their ethereal presence and mysterious character, ghostly apparitions have been a source of intrigue and wonder throughout a wide range of cultures and over the course of history. In spite of the fact that the presence of ghosts and other supernatural phenomena is still a matter of contention, there is a fascinating question that lies at the core of these debates: what are the possible sources of energy that are responsible for ghostly apparitions? In an effort to shed light on the mysteries that surround the potential energy sources that may be the basis for ghostly appearances, this essay investigates a variety of perspectives, ranging from traditional spiritual beliefs to scientific possibilities.

Perspectives on the Spiritual and Metaphysical Existence:

Relative Energy: The concept of residual energy is a belief that is widely embraced in a variety of spiritual and metaphysical traditions. Intense feelings, terrible experiences, or behaviors that are repeated over and over again can sometimes leave an energetic imprint on an area, according to this point of view. It is believed that this residual energy continues to exist, resulting in the formation of a special kind of energetic residue that sensitive individuals are able to perceive or experience. Within the context of this perspective, spectral apparitions could be interpreted as a replay or manifestation of this residual energy.

Spiritual Energy: Numerous religious and spiritual traditions hold the belief that there is an energy that exists beyond the domain of the physical, which is referred to as the soul or spirit. From this point of view, it is possible that ghostly apparitions are manifestations of these spirits who have lost their bodies. According to a number of different belief systems, the energy that maintains the spirit has the potential to interact with the physical world under specific circumstances, which could result in the manifestation of a ghostly presence.

There are a few hypotheses that suggest that people who have heightened psychic talents may be able to emit or interact with energy fields that are beyond the limit of what can be detected by traditional scientific methods. In the context of this discussion, psychic energy has the ability to act as a source for the manifestation of ghostly apparitions. In ways that others are unable to sense or communicate with the spiritual realm, sensitive individuals or mediums who are attuned to these energies may be able to do so.

Positions from the Scientific Community:

Interactions with Quantum Physics: In recent years, a number of scholars have investigated the possibility of linkages between quantum physics and paranormal events, such as the appearance of ghosts. In the field of quantum physics, the concepts of non-locality, entanglement, and the observer effect have been used to propose that the energy dynamics at the quantum level may influence or interact with the macro-scopic world, which could result in the manifestation of ghostly phenomena.

Bioenergetic Fields: Another scientific viewpoint investigates the function of bio-energetic fields, which investigates the potential that living entities, such as people, emit subtle energy fields that can continue to exist after death. In Eastern religions, these fields are frequently associated with ideas such as chi or prana. In theory, these fields could be a contributing factor to the occurrence of ghostly apparitions. It is possible that the residual energy from a person's life force could remain in an area, manifesting as a ghostly presence. This is the premise behind the concept.

Electromagnetic Fields: The influence of electromagnetic fields (EMF) on para-normal events, such as sightings of apparitions, has been the subject of examination among researchers. Whether they are caused by natural or artificial fluctuations in electromagnetic fields, there are theories that suggest that these fluctuations could have an effect on the human brain and perception, resulting in the appearance of ghosts. Those who believe that certain environments with high levels of electromagnetic fields (EMF) are more conducive to having paranormal experiences.

Psychological and Perceptual elements When investigating the possible energy sources that are responsible for ghostly apparitions, it is essential to take into account both psychological and perceptual elements. The experience of ghostly occurrences may be influenced by a number of factors, including abnormalities in brain activity, altered states of consciousness, or increased suggestibility. In this particular setting, the energy is not something that is external but rather something that is the result of internal cognitive processes and sensory experiences.

Investigating the Paranormal and Considering the Perspectives of Technology: Instrumental Measurements People who investigate the paranormal frequently make use of a wide range of devices in order to identify and quantify the probable energy sources that are involved with ghostly apparitions. Infrared cameras, electromagnetic field (EMF) meters, thermographic instruments, and audio recording equipment are all examples of these. In some cases, fluctuations or anomalies that are observed by these equipment are regarded as being indicative of the presence of paranormal energy.

Electronic Voice Phenomena (EVP): EVP, which stands for electronic voice phenomenon, is a phenomenon in which voices or noises that cannot be explained are captured on audio recordings. Virtual reality (EVP) is attributed by some researchers in the field of paranormal studies to possible energy sources associated with spirits or entities that are attempting to communicate. In this particular instance, it is believed that the energy can exert an influence on electronic devices and produce auditory phenomena.

Photographic Anomalies: Photographs that portray anomalies, such as orbs, mists, or light anomalies, are frequently claimed as possible evidence of the existence of paranormal energy sources. Some hypotheses suggest that these peculiar visual occurrences might be the appearance of ghostly apparitions, with the energy interacting with the camera sensors to produce visuals that are out of the ordinary.

Perspectives on Folklore and Cultural Practices:
The cultural forces that are responsible for ghostly apparitions are interpreted in a variety of ways, depending on the cultural and folklore beliefs that accompany them. For the purpose of providing an explanation for ghostly encounters, certain cultures may call particular energies that are considered to be associated with ancestors, nature spirits, or supernatural creatures. The collective beliefs and mythology of a given society are frequently the source of these cultural energies, which are embedded profoundly throughout the community.

There is a concept known as "place memory," which is proposed by certain cultural viewpoints. This concept states that certain areas preserve the energetic imprints of events that occurred in the past. People believe that these impressions, whether they are positive or negative, have the ability to impact the ambiance of a location and may be a contributing factor to the appearance of ghosts. Within the context of this discussion, the energy is connected to the emotional or historical value of a particular site.

Energies from Ceremonial and Ritual procedures Ceremonial and ritual procedures in a variety of cultures involve the purposeful summoning or manipulation of energies. The occurrence of ghostly apparitions during particular rites or ceremonies may be attributed, according to certain cultural beliefs, to the presence of these energies, which may be of a celestial, elemental, or spiritual nature.

Obstacles and Doubts Regarding the Future:

On the other hand, many of the assertions that have been made regarding the origins of paranormal energy do not have any empirical evidence that can withstand the examination of the scientific community. In the absence of evidence that can be independently verified, the veracity of these assertions is obscured.

The interpretation of ghostly apparitions is heavily influenced by the intricacies of human vision, psychology, and cognitive biases. These factors all play a vital part in the interpretation of ghostly apparitions. The perception of paranormal occurrences can be influenced by a number of factors, including optical illusions, pareidolia (the phenomenon of detecting patterns in random data), and persuasion.

Technology Limitations Despite the fact that technical improvements have made paranormal investigations more effective, it is important to recognize that the equipment that is employed has several limitations and defects. False-positive results can be caused by a number of factors, including incorrect interpretations of measurements, mechanical faults, and interferences from the environment.

Personal ideas and Cultural Beliefs: the interpretation of ghostly apparitions is greatly influenced by both personal and cultural ideas. When viewed through the lens of another culture, anything that one culture regards to be a manifestation of spiritual energy may be interpreted quite differently.

Considerations of an Ethical Nature:

Particularly in the context of studies into the paranormal, the research of possible energy sources that could be responsible for ghostly apparitions presents ethical concerns. Responsible researchers are required to:

Try to avoid exploiting people who have had paranormal encounters by making sure that investigations and presentations do not take advantage of the feelings or vulnerabilities of those who have had these experiences.

Respect is maintained by approaching cultural and spiritual beliefs with respect and awareness, avoiding appropriation or misrepresentation of those beliefs where possible.

Transparent Communication: It is important to express the speculative nature of hypotheses and evidence in a clear and concise manner while keeping transparency regarding the challenges that are associated with paranormal phenomena.

Informed Consent: When conducting paranormal investigations, it is important to obtain informed consent from the individuals involved, while also respecting their right to privacy and ensuring their well-being.

An intricate web of beliefs, scientific investigations, and cultural points of view are all intertwined in the investigation of possible energy sources that could be responsible for ghostly apparitions. The mysteries of the paranormal can be viewed through a variety of lenses, ranging from the spiritual and metaphysical worlds to scientific ideas and technical inquiries. Each perspective provides a different lens through which to observe these mysteries.

In spite of the fact that the scientific community continues to regard claims of paranormal activity with caution, the fascination with ghostly apparitions continues to endure. The quest to comprehend the potential energy sources underlying ghostly manifestations pushes us to go into the depths of human experience and the unexplored territory that exist beyond the limitations of our current comprehension. As we navigate the realms of believing and skepticism, we are invited to explore these areas.

3.2 Scientific analysis of reported ectoplasmic phenomena

The concept of ectoplasm, which gained popularity within the realm of spiritualism, has traditionally been linked to spectral manifestations and experiences that are considered to be related to the supernatural. Ectoplasm, which is frequently portrayed as a mysterious and otherworldly substance, has captivated the imaginations of people who are interested in exploring the borders between the natural and supernatural realms during the course of their lives. This article dives into the scientific investigation of ectoplasmic events that have been recorded, analyzing historical settings, attempts to disprove the claims, and the current state of scientific understanding concerning this mysterious substance.

Ectoplasm in the Entire Historical Context:

At the height of spiritualism, which occurred in the latter half of the 19th century and the early 20th century, the idea of ectoplasm came into being. persons who claimed to interact with spirits, typically via the use of séances, referred to ectoplasm as a substance that was emitted by mediums. These persons believed that ectoplasm served as a bridge between the physical and spiritual realms. Mediums would enter trance states, and it was stated that during these sessions, ectoplasmic manifestations would take place. The substance would take on a variety of forms, such as mist, tendrils, or even solid formations.

Eva C. and Kluski, two prominent characters in the spiritualist movement, received prominence for their alleged capacity to produce ectoplasmic occurrences. This talent was a source of fascination for many people. Photographic evidence from séances frequently depicted these mediums surrounded by the mystery substance, which contributed to the widespread acceptance of ectoplasmic appearances.

Defeating Attempts and Skepticism:

As ectoplasmic occurrences garnered more attention from the general public, they also became the focus of scientific investigation and experiments that attempted to disprove them. Skeptics and researchers were interested in determining whether or not the substance in question was a genuine manifestation of the paranormal or whether it was a product of fraud. They wanted to explore the veracity of the ectoplasmic occurrences that were reported.

Exposures Made by Harry Houdini Harry Houdini, a well-known escape artist and magician, was a famous skeptic of spiritualist practices. He aggressively attempted to expose fraudulent mediums and ectoplasmic phenomena at the time. In the course of his studies, which were frequently carried out in conjunction with scientific experts, Houdini discovered cases of deception. These instances involved mediums employing materials such as cheesecloth, muslin, or substances that had been regurgitated in order to give the impression of ectoplasm.

Photographic Manipulation: In addition, photographic evidence of ectoplasmic appearances was investigated and analyzed. It was suggested by critics that certain media and photographers manipulated photos by employing techniques like double exposure, darkroom procedures, or the deliberate use of materials in order to produce the illusion of ectoplasm. The disclosure of such manipulations was a contributing factor in the development of an increasing level of doubt regarding the legitimacy of ectoplasmic events.

Exposure of Fraudulent Mediums: When a number of mediums that claimed to produce ectoplasm were revealed to be fraudulent, the credibility of these phenomena was severely undermined. There have been instances in which mediums have been apprehended by employing techniques such as sleight of hand, disguised materials, or other deceptive methods in order to create the illusion of ectoplasmic phenomena.

Investigations of Ectoplasm Based on Scientific Research:

Researchers in the modern era have taken a more nuanced approach to the study of ectoplasmic occurrences, in contrast to the early scientific inquiries, which frequently concentrated on exposing fraudulent methods. In recent years, scientific methodologies and technical breakthroughs have made it possible to conduct a more comprehensive investigation of the ectoplasmic manifestations that have been reported, taking into account both the psychological and physical components of the phenomenon.

Within the realm of contemporary study, the involvement of psychological elements in the experience of ectoplasmic events is recognized and acknowledged. Cognitive biases, suggestibility, and the power of suggestion are all factors that can have a substantial impact on how individuals interpret and experience paranormal occurrences.

It is essential to have a proper understanding of the psychological features in order to differentiate between experiences that are authentic and those that are impacted by subjective factors.

Environmental conditions: Present-day investigators of the paranormal frequently take into consideration environmental conditions that could be a contributing factor to ectoplasmic events that have been documented. In the course of paranormal investigations, fluctuations in electromagnetic fields (EMF), temperature, and humidity are among the variables that are investigated in order to ascertain the potential impact that these variables may have on perceptions and experiences.

Analysis of Technology: Recent developments in technology have made it possible to acquire new instruments for conducting scientific research on ectoplasmic occurrences that have been recorded. During investigations into the paranormal, various imaging instruments, such as infrared cameras, full-spectrum cameras, and others, are utilized to record any visual anomalies that may be present. Researchers have the ability to document and study occurrences that may be invisible to the naked eye thanks to the technologies that are available to them.

Neuroscientific Studies: In an effort to gain a better understanding of the brain systems that are responsible for paranormal experiences, a number of researchers have delved into neuroscientific studies. Through the analysis of brain activity and responses during reported contacts with ectoplasmic phenomena, the objective of the scientists is to find patterns that have the potential to shed light on the neurological processes that are connected with subjective experiences of the paranormal.

Natural explanations for ectoplasmic phenomena that have been reported and discussed:

Pareidolia and Pattern Recognition: The tendency of the human brain to recognize recognizable patterns or faces in random stimuli is known as pareidolia. This tendency may be a factor in the interpretation of visual abnormalities as ectoplasmic occurrences. During inquiries into the paranormal, those who are experiencing heightened emotional states or anticipation may be more prone to experiencing pareidolia.

Situations of Low Light: Many ectoplasmic manifestations have been reported to take place under low-light situations, such as those that are present during séances or investigations into the paranormal. When visibility is reduced, it might be difficult to appropriately perceive and interpret visual inputs, which can result in the incorrect identification of commonplace objects or phenomena as ectoplasm.

Mist and other meteorological circumstances contribute to visual anomalies that may be interpreted as ectoplasm. Mist, fog, and other atmospheric variables can all contribute to these kinds of aberrations. When natural environmental variables are mixed with a psychological propensity to detect paranormal phenomena, the result might be a setting that is conducive to the misunderstanding of everyday happenings.

Certain physiological factors, such as heightened emotional states, tension, or weariness, might alter perception and contribute to the reporting of paranormal encounters. Furthermore, certain physiological variables can also play a role in the occurrence of paranormal experiences. To determine the origin of such reports, it is essential to have a solid understanding of the interaction that exists between biological elements and the ectoplasmic occurrences that have been recorded.

Taking into Account Ethical Considerations When Conducting Scientific Research:

By providing their informed consent, individuals who take part in paranormal investigations should demonstrate that they have a thorough awareness of the nature of the research as well as the potential psychological or emotional consequence of their participation.

Respect for Believers: Researchers have a responsibility to approach the topic with respect for people who have genuine beliefs in the existence of paranormal events. When it comes to sustaining ethical research techniques, striking a balance between skepticism and empathy was vital.

Transparency in Reporting: When doing scientific research on ectoplasmic occurrences, it is essential to report findings in a transparent manner. It is important for researchers to clarify the methodologies that were utilized, as well as any potential limitations and the speculative nature of interpretations.

For the sake of responsible research, it is imperative that researchers refrain from taking advantage of the feelings or vulnerabilities of individuals who have had experiences that are considered to be paranormal. It is crucial to have sensitivity to the potentially deep impact that persons' beliefs in the paranormal can have on them.

The scientific investigation of ectoplasmic occurrences that have been reported is an example of a multi-faceted investigation that takes into account historical settings, attempts to disprove the phenomenon, and contemporary research approaches.

Although the idea of ectoplasm originated within the spiritualist movement and has been linked to ideas in the paranormal, scientific research are currently being conducted in an effort to discover the mysteries that lie behind the phenomena that have been observed.

Skepticism, open-mindedness, and ethical considerations are the three pillars that modern researchers employ when they approach the study of ectoplasmic manifestations. The incorporation of psychological, environmental, and technological assessments adds to a more thorough understanding of ectoplasmic occurrences that have been observed. This approach acknowledges the intricacies of human perception as well as the possibility of natural answers.

As scientific inquiry continues to advance, the investigation of reported ectoplasmic phenomena presents researchers with the opportunity to navigate the delicate balance between skepticism and curiosity. This allows them to shed light on the nature of reported paranormal experiences while simultaneously respecting the various perspectives and beliefs that contribute to the enduring mystique of ectoplasm.

3.3 Exploring the correlation between energy fields and apparitional manifestations

Various theoretical frameworks have been explored by researchers and enthusiasts in order to gain a better understanding of the mysterious nature of apparitional manifestations. This is because the junction of paranormal occurrences and scientific inquiry has led to this intersection. The examination of the association between energy fields and the incidence of apparitions is a fascinating path of inquiry that may be pursued more thoroughly. This essay dives into the investigation of this association, taking into account both traditional spiritual beliefs and contemporary scientific perspectives, with the goal of elucidating the possible connections that exist between energy fields and the appearance of apparitions.

Beliefs in Traditional Spiritual Practices:

Spiritual Energy: Traditional spiritual beliefs postulate the existence of spiritual energy that is not limited to the domain of the physical. It is commonly thought that this energy, which is associated with the soul or spirit, continues to exist after a person's physical death. A connection between the spiritual and material worlds is represented by apparitions, which are regarded to be representations of the spiritual energy that is being discussed here.

Some spiritual traditions believe that intense feelings, terrible experiences, or deeds that are repeated over and over again can leave behind imprints of residual energy in a particular spot. It is believed that these impressions will never disappear and will continue to have an effect on the surrounding environment, which may result in the appearance of apparitions.

It is claimed that the residual energy manages to preserve certain characteristics of the past, thereby enabling individuals to experience scenes from bygone eras.

The term "psychic energy" refers to a sort of subtle energy that is known to be related with awareness and psychic skills, as stated by spiritual beliefs. Individuals who have a heightened psychic sensitivity may be able to feel or interact with this energy, which may facilitate the manifestation of apparitions, according to certain views. In instance, it is thought that psychic mediums are able to harness and channel psychic energy in order to interact with afterlife entities.

Perspectives from the Scientific Community on Energy Fields:

Electromagnetic Fields (EMF): One scientific approach studies the association between electromagnetic fields (EMF) and apparitional occurrences. The electromagnetic field that is produced by the human body is relatively faint but may be measured, and certain situations may exhibit oscillations in the electromagnetic field (EMF). These fluctuations could be linked to the manifestation of apparitions, according to the hypothesis of certain researchers who study the paranormal. This hypothesis suggests that these fluctuations could be caused by the manipulation or interaction of electromagnetic fields by spirits or beings.

Bioenergetic Fields: The term "bioenergetic fields" refers to the subtle energy that is believed to flow within living creatures. Additionally, in Eastern traditions, bioenergetic fields are frequently related with ideas such as chi or prana. Within the realm of science, researchers have investigated the possibility that individuals may radiate bioenergetic fields that have the potential to have an effect on the surrounding environment. The interplay between these fields and the environment is thought to play a role in the manifestation of apparitions, according to one theory.

Interactions of Quantum Physics: Quantum physics, with its principles of non-locality, entanglement, and the observer effect, has been invoked in order to investigate the possibility of linkages between energy fields and apparitions. In the realm of paranormal phenomena, proponents of quantum perspectives propose that the manipulation of quantum states or the effect of consciousness on the quantum level could potentially serve as a theoretical foundation for the manifestation of apparitions.

The Function of Energy Fields in the Manifestations of Apparitional Aspects:

Energy Resonance: The idea of energy resonance suggests that particular areas may resonate with particular energies that are related with previous occurrences, feelings, or individuals. It is possible that, according to this theory, apparitions are manifestations of energies that resonate with a specific location or certain instant in time.

It is possible for persons who are sensitive or who are attuned to these energies to experience apparitions as a consequence of resonance frequencies.

Transfer of Energy: There are hypotheses that propose that apparitions may draw upon external energy sources in order to materialize out of thin air. There is a theory that suggests that the materialization of apparitions is influenced by the transmission of energy from the surroundings, live individuals, or other things. When viewed from this angle, the concept that spirits or beings control available energy in order to interact with the physical world is consistent with this viewpoint.

Apparitional manifestations are frequently recorded in particular environmental conditions, such as sites with high amounts of atmospheric electricity, geomagnetic anomalies, or other energy-related phenomena. These conditions can be found in a variety of settings. It is possible that gaining an understanding of the potential function that energy fields play in paranormal experiences can be accomplished by doing research into the association between the environmental energy conditions and the appearance of apparitions.

Instrumental Measurements and Technological Advancements:

EMF Meters and Environmental Sensors: In order to identify oscillations in energy fields, electromagnetic field (EMF) meters and environmental sensors are frequently utilized by paranormal investigators during the course of their investigations. A number of people are of the opinion that the occurrence of apparitions is correlated with increases in EMF readings. Skepticism, on the other hand, is prevalent among the scientific community, which highlights the significance of taking into consideration other explanations for oscillations of this kind.

Infrared and Full-Spectrum Cameras: Recent developments in technology have made it possible for infrared and full-spectrum cameras to be utilized in the field of paranormal investigations. In order to potentially uncover anomalies that are connected with apparitional manifestations, these devices are able to gather visual data that extends beyond the range of human eyesight. The analysis of this visual data, in conjunction with measurements of the surrounding environment, adds to a more comprehensive knowledge of the potential relationships between electromagnetic fields.

Audio Recording equipment: Electronic voice phenomena (EVP), which are acquired by audio recording equipment during investigations of the paranormal, are sometimes regarded to be evidence of communication with spirits. An approach that is taken in the investigation of strange sounds or voices is based on the hypothesis that energy fields have the potential to impact electrical devices, which can result in auditory phenomena that cannot be explained.

Obstacles and Doubts Regarding the Future:

A lack of standardization presents difficulties in understanding and reproducing the results of paranormal investigations because there are no established standards for conducting such investigations. The formation of standard scientific methods is hampered by the fact that various investigators use a wide variety of methodologies and pieces of equipment.

Comparison of Correlation and Causation: It is difficult to establish a direct causal relationship between energy fields and apparitional manifestations. The observation of correlations is possible; nevertheless, in order to attribute causation, one must have solid empirical evidence and controlled experiments, both of which are frequently absent in studies on the paranormal.

There are a number of psychological aspects that play a big part in the experience of apparitions. Some of these factors include cognitive biases, suggestion, and the power of believing. There is a possibility that these elements will have an impact on the interpretation of energy field measurements and will contribute to the correlation that has been recorded between energy fields and paranormal instances.

Considerations of an Ethical Nature:

Individuals who take part in paranormal investigations are required to give their informed consent, which means they must be aware of the potential psychological and emotional effects that the research may have on them.

Respect for Believers: Researchers have a responsibility to approach the topic with respect for people who have genuine beliefs in the existence of paranormal events. Keeping a healthy equilibrium between skepticism and empathy is essential for conducting research in an ethical manner.

Transparency in Reporting: When doing scientific research on energy fields and apparitional manifestations, it is absolutely necessary to report findings in a transparent manner. It is important for researchers to clearly clarify the methodologies that were utilized, as well as any potential limitations and the speculative nature of interpretations.

For the sake of responsible research, it is imperative that researchers refrain from taking advantage of the feelings or vulnerabilities of individuals who have had experiences that are considered to be paranormal. It is crucial to have sensitivity to the potentially deep impact that persons' beliefs in the paranormal can have on them.

It is an interesting and complex study that spans traditional spiritual beliefs, scientific perspectives, and technology breakthroughs. The investigation of the association between energy fields and apparitional phenomena is a fascinating and multidimensional inquiry. On the other hand, contemporary research investigates the relationships between electromagnetic fields, bioenergetic fields, and quantum interactions. Traditional beliefs ascribe apparitions to spiritual or psychic energy.

The discourse between the scientific community and the paranormal community is currently continuing, and scientific investigations that are done with ethical considerations and transparency contribute to this dialogue. In the process of navigating the complexity of energy fields and apparitional appearances, researchers are bridging the gap between the known and the unknown. They are encouraging us to examine the mysteries that lay at the crossroads of the tangible and the ethereal.

Chapter 4

EMF and Spirits: Unraveling the Electric Connections

For a very long time, the domain of the paranormal has been able to captivate the imagination of humans, which has resulted in the development of a multitude of beliefs, myths, and ideas concerning the existence of spirits or beings that are beyond our comprehension. It is believed that there is a connection between electromagnetic fields (EMF) and spiritual experiences, which is an intriguing part of this mystical universe. The purpose of this investigation is to investigate the electromagnetic field (EMF) and spirits, with the objective of elucidating the electric links that some people assert exist between the unseen and the electromagnetic spectrum.

Electromagnetic Fields (EMF) Understanding and Understanding

Prior to going into the supposed connections between electromagnetic fields and spirits, it is essential to have a fundamental understanding of electromagnetic fields. One of the most fundamental aspects of physics is the concept of electromagnetic fields, which are symbolic representations of the combined electric and magnetic fields that are produced by charged particles. There is a spectrum of these fields, which ranges from low-frequency fields, like those produced by power lines, to high-frequency fields, like those connected with radio waves and visible light. Each of these fields has its own unique characteristics.

The electromagnetic field (EMF) is emitted by a variety of equipment in our technologically advanced society. These devices include power lines, electrical appliances, and wireless communication technology. Extensive study has been conducted as a result of concerns regarding the potential adverse health effects of extended exposure to electromagnetic fields (EMF). However, the findings of this research have been unclear and frequently controversial.

EMF and Other Experiences of the Paranormal

With the emergence of ghost hunting and paranormal research, the idea that electromagnetic fields (EMF) might be connected to paranormal events, such as encounters with spirits or ghosts, gained popularity. In the course of their investigations, ghost hunters frequently make use of electromagnetic field meters, which are also referred to as EMF meters, in order to identify any shifts in the electromagnetic environment that is present.

Some people who are interested in the paranormal believe that spirits, because they are made up of energy, have the ability to influence or create electromagnetic fields. It is the contention of those who support this hypothesis that increases in electromagnetic field measurements that occur during ghost hunts might be an indication of the existence of a spiritual being. Skeptics, on the other side, believe that these fluctuations are caused by natural ambient variables, electrical wiring, or the gadgets themselves.

Haunted Places and Electromagnetic Field Readings

Elevated electromagnetic field readings have been shown to be connected with a number of supposedly haunted places. As an illustration, it is commonly believed that older buildings that have wiring that is not functioning properly or historical places that have leftover energy are more likely to be affected by paranormal activity. Both the scientific community and the paranormal community have been spurred by discussions regarding the claimed association between high levels of electromagnetic fields (EMF) and ghostly encounters.

The investigation of the paranormal and electromagnetic fields

Research into the relationship between electromagnetic fields (EMF) and supernatural occurrences has been limited and has not produced solid results. It has been argued that the techniques and interpretations of certain studies have been questioned for their lack of rigor and scientific validity, despite the fact that some studies have revealed connections between high EMF levels and accounts of paranormal encounters.

When conducting study on the paranormal, one of the challenges that can arise is the subjective character of human encounters. Some people believe that anecdotal evidence is not reliable because it is frequently impacted by psychological variables, suggestibility, and cultural views. Skeptics contend that this is the case. Although there are obstacles to overcome, there is a persistent interest in bridging the gap between the scientific community and the paranormal community in order to investigate the possible connections between electromagnetic fields (EMF) and spiritual encounters.

Understanding the EMF-Spirit Connection Through Various Theories

The putative connection between electromagnetic fields (EMF) and spirits has been the subject of multiple hypotheses and explanations. Despite the fact that these theories are based on speculation and do not have any empirical evidence to back them up, they provide intriguing insights on the junction of the physical and spiritual domains.

The Theory of Energy Residues

Emotional energy, particularly the deep feelings that are linked with traumatic experiences, is something that can leave a residual impression on the surroundings, according to a notion that is widely accepted. It is hypothesized that these emotional imprints have the ability to interact with or impact electromagnetic fields, generating conditions that are favorable to the occurrence of paranormal events. As a result of the possibility that they maintain this leftover energy, places that have a history of violence, tragedy, or extreme emotions are sometimes regarded to have a higher probability of being haunted.

Theory of the Manifestation of Spirit

Some people who believe in the relationship between electromagnetic fields and spirits believe that spirits, who are energy entities, are able to influence electromagnetic fields in order to make their presence known. This idea proposes that spirits draw on the energy that is present in their surroundings in order to express themselves in ways that are observable by living beings. These manifestations may take the form of apparitions, auditory occurrences, or changes in the electromagnetic environment. Despite this, there is still a huge obstacle to overcome for this idea, and that is the absence of tangible evidence that supports such manifestations.

The Entanglement of Quantum

A theory that is more speculative and controversial from a scientific standpoint is one that is based on the principles of quantum mechanics. The phenomenon known as quantum entanglement, which is discovered at the subatomic level, shows that particles can become entangled and influence each other's states whether or not they are physically separated from one another. The existence of consciousness or spiritual entities within a quantum realm, which may influence or interact with the physical world through quantum entanglement, is a theory that has been proposed by some individuals over the years. Despite the fact that it is intriguing, this hypothesis is very theoretical and does not have any empirical evidence within the paradigm of quantum mechanics that is now understood.

Points of View That Are Skeptical Regarding EMF and Spirits

Factors Relating to Psychology

There are others who believe that many paranormal experiences can be explained by psychological variables, such as the power of belief, suggestion, and expectation. Skeptics claim that this is the case. Individuals may interpret normal environmental cues as paranormal phenomena, particularly in areas associated with ghost stories or urban legends. This is because the human brain is very receptive to suggestion, including the ability to interpret typical environmental stimuli.

Variables in the Environment

It is common practice to blame high electromagnetic field (EMF) levels in reputedly haunted locales on faulty wiring, electrical equipment, or natural geomagnetic swings and fluctuations. Skeptics argue that changes in electromagnetic field measurements can be caused by sources that are more ordinary and can be explained, rather than being the result of the influence of spiritual entities.

Restriction of the Equipment

The limitations of such equipment are brought up by those who are opposed to the usage of techniques for investigating the paranormal, including the utilization of EMF meters. Meters that measure electromagnetic fields (EMF) are sensitive to a wide range of electromagnetic sources, such as power lines, electronic gadgets, and electric appliances found in the home. It is possible for the equipment itself or other variables that are unrelated to paranormal activity to cause false positives or anomalies in results.

Social and cultural influences on the world

The way people perceive the supernatural is significantly influenced by their cultural beliefs as well as the social environment in which they live. Those who are skeptical of the supernatural believe that the widespread use of ghost stories, horror films, and cultural narratives about spirits are factors that contribute to the perception of anomalous events as being supernatural. It is possible for individuals to detect paranormal occurrences in situations when none may actually exist, because of the power of suggestion, which is fed by societal expectations.

Scientific Research and Electromagnetic Fields

There are some researchers who have conducted systematic examinations to investigate the potential connections between electromagnetic fields (EMF) and paranormal experiences. This is despite the fact that skepticism is an essential component of scientific inquiry. Methodological problems, ethical considerations, and the inherent difficulty of analyzing subjective experiences are frequently encountered in these types of investigations. In spite of these challenges, the scientific investigations that have been conducted into the connection between electromagnetic fields (EMF) and the supernatural have produced some fascinating discoveries.

Conducting Field Research in Haunted Locations

Field studies have been carried out by researchers in areas that are rumored to be haunted in order to quantify electromagnetic fields (EMF) levels and connect them with alleged paranormal experiences. Several investigations have found a correlation between high electromagnetic field (EMF) readings and cases of ghostly activity that have been reported. On the other hand, these findings are not conclusive because it is not possible to rule out other possible reasons, such as ambient influences or artifacts from the equipment.

Studies That Are Under Control

Experimentally controlled trials have been devised to study the impact of electromagnetic fields (EMF) on human perception and experience. This is done in order to solve the limitations of field investigations. The volunteers in these tests are frequently subjected to regulated electromagnetic fields, and their experiences are evaluated based on what they claim having experienced. There is an association between exposure to electromagnetic fields (EMF) and altered states of consciousness, according to certain research; however, the results of these studies are inconsistent, and the processes that are responsible for such effects are yet unknown.

Perspectives on Neurological and Cognitive Functioning

Researchers have investigated the notion that being exposed to particular electromagnetic fields could have an effect on the brain and the cognitive processes that occur within it, which could potentially result in changed perceptions or experiences that are not conventional. Due to the complexity of the link between electromagnetic fields

(EMF) and the brain, the scientific community has not yet arrived at an agreement regarding the exact effects that electromagnetic fields have on human consciousness.

Regarding the Ethical Implications of Research on the Paranormal

There are ethical concerns that arise while conducting research on paranormal occurrences, such as the possible relationship between electromagnetic fields (EMF) and spirits. These concerns include the well-being of the participants, the need for informed consent, and the possibility of psychological injury. When conducting research in this area, researchers have the responsibility of striking a balance between conducting scientific inquiries and considering the potential impact their findings may have on those who are susceptible to being influenced or distressed.

Concerns have also been raised over the ethical treatment of the subject matter as a result of the portrayal of paranormal investigations in the media, such as reality television shows that are centered on ghost hunting. When doing research and investigations, it is important to keep in mind the possibility of sensationalism as well as the influence that media portrayal has on how the general public views the supernatural.

The interaction between electromagnetic fields with the world of the paranormal continues to be a fascinating and mysterious area of investigation. Although there are glimpses into the potential connections between electromagnetic fields (EMF) and spirits that may be found in anecdotal reports, field investigations, and controlled tests, definitive evidence is still difficult to come by. Proponents of the electromagnetic field (EMF)-spirit connection continue to investigate alternate explanations, while skeptics maintain that psychological, environmental, and technological elements can account for reported paranormal experiences.

When attempting to gain an understanding of the riddles surrounding the paranormal, it is necessary to take a multidisciplinary approach that integrates rigorous scientific methodologies, open-minded research, and ethical considerations. It is likely that the search to untangle the electric links between electromagnetic fields (EMF) and spirits will continue to fascinate the curiosity of both believers and skeptics alike as technology continues to progress and our grasp of the electromagnetic spectrum continues to deepen. In the intricate dynamic that exists between the visible and the invisible, the investigation of the unknown continues to be a human activity that has stood the test of time.

4.1 Investigating the role of electromagnetic fields in ghostly encounters

The domain of the supernatural has long been a source of interest, with ghostly encounters and paranormal experiences attracting the imagination of humans across a wide range of cultures and time periods. In the past several years, there has been an increasing interest in investigating the possibility of a relationship between electromagnetic fields (EMF) and spectral phenomena. The purpose of this inquiry is to investigate the role that electromagnetic fields play in ghostly encounters. Specifically, the investigation will look at the hypotheses, empirical research, and arguments that surround this fascinating convergence of the physical and the metaphysical.

Electromagnetic Fields (EMF) Understanding and Understanding

It is crucial to have a thorough understanding of what electromagnetic fields involve before delving into the precise relationship between electromagnetic fields and ghostly encounters. This information is necessary before engaging in the investigation. The electromagnetic fields that are formed by charged particles are a fundamental component of the study of physics. These fields include both the electric and magnetic fields themselves. Different frequencies of these fields can be found over a spectrum, ranging from low-frequency fields that are generated by power lines to high-frequency fields that are connected with radio waves and visible light.

The electromagnetic field (EMF) is emitted by a wide variety of devices and technology in our contemporary world. These include power lines, domestic appliances, and wireless communication gadgets. Despite the fact that the scientific community has not yet arrived at an agreement on the subject, substantial research has been conducted as a result of concerns regarding the potential adverse health effects that could result from continuous exposure to electromagnetic fields.

An Examination of the Historical Context of Ghostly Encounters

Throughout the course of human history, there have been documented accounts of ghostly encounters and supernatural occurrences. These accounts have transcended both cultural and geographical boundaries.

Despite the fact that these tales frequently differ in terms of specifics, recurring themes include apparitions, unseen sounds, and disturbances that cannot be explained. These experiences have been interpreted in a variety of ways over the course of time, with cultural, religious, and societal views playing a significant role.

Ancient cultures frequently attributed encounters with ghosts to divine intervention, ancestral spirits, or supernatural powers. These explanations were common in ancient cultures. Alternative explanations for paranormal experiences evolved as cultures advanced and scientific understanding advanced. These explanations ranged from psychological phenomena to natural environmental variables and included a variety of different factors.

Developments in the Fields of Ghost Hunting and Investigations of the Paranormal

The 19th and 20th century saw an increase in the number of organized initiatives to research and document occurrences that were considered to be paranormal. Spiritualism, occult practices, and a growing interest in the unknown all served as sources of inspiration for the development of the field of ghost hunting. When conducting their investigations, early ghost hunters frequently relied on individuals' personal experiences, mythology, and the guidance of spiritual mediums.

As technology progressed, the tools that were accessible to those who investigated the paranormal also advanced. Electromagnetic field meters, often known as EMF meters, have become increasingly common among these instruments for the purpose of detecting changes in the electromagnetic environment present in the surrounding area during investigations. This development in technology signaled a transition from evidence that was solely anecdotal and subjective to the incorporation of scientific tools in the effort to gain a better understanding of ghostly encounters.

Theories that Link Electromagnetic Fields with Ghostly Phenomena

A number of hypotheses have been proposed in an effort to provide an explanation for the possible connection between electromagnetic fields and ghostly encounters. These hypotheses, despite the fact that they frequently lack scientific backing, contribute to the ongoing discourse on the nature of experiences that are considered to be paranormal.

Theory of the Manifestation of Energy

The idea that ghosts or spirits, which are made up of energy, are able to influence or present themselves through the interaction with electromagnetic fields is a hypothesis that is widely accepted. As a result of changes in electromagnetic field readings during ghost hunts, proponents of this theory say that spirits draw upon the energy that is present in their surroundings in order to manifest in ways that are observable to living people.

This theory functions under the assumption that there is a direct connection between the energy of a spirit and the electromagnetic fields that it is said to impact.

Impression of Remaining Electrons

On the basis of the concept of residual energy imprints, it is postulated that traumatic or intensely emotional experiences might leave an energetic trace on the surrounding environment. This emotional energy is said to interact with electromagnetic fields, which could potentially result in ghostly appearances or other events that are considered to be otherworldly. It is commonly believed that individuals are more prone to exhibit these lingering energy imprints in locations that have a history of experiencing violence, tragedy, or emotional intensity.

The Entanglement of Quantum

In a more speculative hypothesis, the laws of quantum physics serve as a source of inspiration, and the theory proposes that consciousness or spiritual entities can be found within a quantum realm. A connection between the world of the living and the realm of the spirit may be possible, according to this idea, because quantum entanglement, which is a phenomenon that can be witnessed at the subatomic level, may make it possible. In spite of the fact that it is intriguing, this hypothesis is still extremely speculative and does not have any empirical validity within the framework of the available knowledge regarding quantum mechanics.

Scientific Investigations into Electromagnetic Fields and Other Paranormal Occurrences

There has been a relatively new trend in the realm of science that investigates the connection between electromagnetic fields and ghostly encounters. Studies have been carried out by researchers in order to evaluate the possibility of links between unusual electromagnetic readings and instances of paranormal experiences that have been reported. However, there is still a lack of consensus among members of the scientific community regarding the validity and interpretation of these findings.

Conducting Field Research in Haunted Locations

Some researchers have carried out field study in areas that are rumored to be haunted, measuring the levels of electromagnetic fields while simultaneously documenting the experiences that have been alleged to be had by the paranormal. This research endeavors to determine whether or if there is a connection between variations in electromagnetic field readings and occurrences of ghostly activity. Critics contend that the diversity of contextual elements and the subjective character of paranormal experiences provide obstacles in demonstrating causation, despite the fact that some data imply a connection between the two.

Studies That Are Under Control

Experimental methods that are controlled have been developed in order to investigate the effects of electromagnetic fields on human perception and experience. This is done in order to address the limitations of field investigations. These tests frequently involve subjecting subjects to controlled electromagnetic field (EMF) conditions and evaluating the experiences that they have described. Despite the fact that certain studies have found links between exposure to electromagnetic fields (EMF) and altered states of consciousness, the findings continue to be inconsistent, and the processes that are responsible for these correlations are not fully understood.

Perspectives on Neurological and Cognitive Functioning

Researchers have also investigated the possibility that electromagnetic fields could have an effect on the human brain and the cognitive processes that occur within it. The purpose of the research being conducted in this field is to identify whether or not being exposed to particular electromagnetic frequencies might cause altered states of consciousness or perceptual anomalies, which could potentially contribute to the occurrence of ghostly encounters. There is a complicated interaction between electromagnetic fields (EMF) and the brain, and research in this area is still ongoing.

Speculative Perspectives on Electromagnetic Fields and Ghostly Encounters

Despite the fact that there is a lot of interest in the topic and there have been some discoveries that are suggestive, the scientific community continues to be skeptical about the supposed connections between electromagnetic fields and ghostly encounters. Skeptics contest the validity of these linkages by bringing up various crucial arguments, including the following:

Reasons Based on Psychological Theory

There are others who believe that many paranormal experiences can be explained by psychological variables, such as the power of belief, suggestion, and expectation. Skeptics claim that this is the case. It is possible for individuals to interpret normal environmental inputs as paranormal activities, particularly in environments that are connected with ghost stories or urban legends. This is because human perception is prone to cognitive biases.

Variables in the Environment

In places that are said to be haunted, high levels of electromagnetic fields are sometimes attributed to non-spiritual causes, such as defective wiring, electronic gadgets, or natural geomagnetic changes. Skeptics underline the significance of taking ambient elements into consideration before attributing aberrant readings to ghostly activities. This is because fluctuations in electromagnetic field measurements might occur for reasons that are unrelated to paranormal activity.

Restriction of the Equipment

The limitations of such equipment are brought to light by those who are opposed to the usage of techniques for investigating the paranormal, including the utilization of EMF meters. False positives or anomalies in readings may be caused by the equipment itself or by external circumstances that are unrelated to paranormal activity. Electromagnetic field meters are sensitive to a wide range of electromagnetic sources. Skeptics emphasize the importance of taking stringent calibration and control methods while conducting research into the paranormal.

Social and cultural influences on the world

The cultural and social environment in which paranormal investigations are conducted can have a considerable impact on how experiences are perceived and how they are interpreted with regard to those experiences. Skeptics contend that the proliferation of ghost stories, horror movies, and cultural narratives about spirits can contribute to the interpretation of anomalous events as being supernatural. They say this because these narratives are widespread. It is possible for individuals to detect paranormal occurrences in situations when none may actually exist, because of the power of suggestion, which is fed by societal expectations.

Considerations of an Ethical Nature in the Investigation of Ghostly Phenomena

The investigation of ghostly encounters and other paranormal occurrences requires researchers and investigators to negotiate the ethical problems that arise as a result of these investigations. When confronted with potentially uncomfortable or unexplained experiences, participants in studies or investigations may be susceptible to suggestion, distress, or anxiety. This is especially true when the participants are exposed to the experiences. In paranormal research, it is of the utmost importance to uphold ethical standards, obtain informed consent from participants, and ensure their well-being.

Concerns have also been expressed over sensationalism and the potential impact on popular conceptions of the paranormal as a result of the representation of ghost hunting in the media, such as in reality television shows and documentaries. The portrayal of paranormal investigations in a responsible and ethical manner is vital in order to avoid the perpetuation of misinformation or the exploitation of the fear that is connected with experiencing ghostly encounters.

Towards the Future of Research Directions

Observations Made Over Time

There is a possibility that longitudinal studies that observe and measure oscillations in electromagnetic fields over extended periods of time in areas that are rumored to be haunted could yield significant information.

The results of such investigations would be helpful in distinguishing between environmental influences that are fleeting and those that are persistent and could be associated with strange occurrences.

Imaging Methods That Are More Advanced

Recent developments in imaging technologies, including thermal imaging and infrared cameras, have the potential to improve our capacity to record and record abnormal occurrences that are connected with ghostly encounters that have been recorded. When these technologies are combined with electromagnetic field (EMF) measurements, it is possible that a more comprehensive knowledge of the interaction between the electromagnetic environment and claimed paranormal activity can be brought about.

Studies That Go Across Cultures

The cultural variables that determine people's experiences of ghostly encounters could be better understood by comparative research that draws from a variety of various cultures and belief systems. In order to contribute to a more nuanced and interdisciplinary approach to the study of the paranormal, it may be beneficial to get an understanding of how the cultural environment influences the interpretation of anomalous events.

Cooperation with Neuroscientists and Researchers

It is possible that the potential connections between electromagnetic fields and altered states of consciousness could be further investigated through the collaboration of neuroscientists and investigators of the human paranormal. It is possible that gaining an understanding of the cognitive processes that lead to ghostly encounters can be accomplished through the investigation of the neurological underpinnings of such experiences.

An intriguing combination of science, mythology, and the unexplained is being explored through the research of the role that electromagnetic fields play in ghostly encounters. Despite the fact that anecdotal accounts, field investigations, and controlled tests provide insights into probable linkages, the scientific community has not yet arrived at an agreement regarding the nature of these occurrences.

When it comes to analyzing alleged ghostly encounters, skeptics stress the significance of taking into account psychological, environmental, and technical elements. In the field of paranormal research, the importance of maintaining a balanced and cautious approach cannot be overstated on account of the ethical considerations involving the well-being of participants and appropriate media depiction.

There is a good chance that the investigation into the mysteries of ghostly experiences will continue as technology continues to progress and our grasp of the electromagnetic spectrum continues to get deeper. It is a monument to humanity's continuing interest and the ongoing effort to understand the unexplainable that the exploration of this mysterious region acts as a testament.

4.2 EMF meters and their relevance in paranormal research

Electromagnetic field (EMF) meters have become extremely commonplace in the field of paranormal investigation. These meters are utilized to detect and analyze oscillations in the electromagnetic environment that is surrounding the subject. Researchers that are interested in investigating the possible connections between electromagnetic fields and paranormal occurrences have shown a growing interest in these devices, which have acquired popularity among ghost hunters, paranormal enthusiasts, and researchers. This in-depth investigation looks into the realm of electromagnetic field meters (EMF meters), analyzing their technology, their use in the field of paranormal research, the controversies that surround them, and the current arguments that surround their significance in the pursuit of understanding the mysteries of the paranormal.

Acquiring Knowledge on EMF Meters

The Fundamentals of the Business:

Electromagnetic field (EMF) meters analyze the electromagnetic field that surrounds the device in order to identify any changes that may occur. Changes in the electromagnetic environment are frequently signaled by variations in the readings of the meter, with spikes or fluctuations indicating that an alteration has occurred in the electromagnetic environment. Single-axis and tri-axis models are the most popular types of electromagnetic field meters. The latter form of EMF meter has the capability to detect electromagnetic fields in many directions at the same time during the measurement process.

Electromagnetic Fields Can Look Like These:

Measuring both static and dynamic electromagnetic fields is the purpose of electromagnetic field meters (EMF meters). Static fields, which are often referred to as direct current (DC) fields, are fields that tend to remain constant and are typically connected with natural sources such as the magnetic field of the Earth. Alternating current (AC) fields, also known as dynamic fields, are characterized by their fluctuating strength and are typically generated by electrical equipment, power lines, and other sources that are considered to be man-made.

Utilizations Outside of the Field of Paranormal Research:

Electromagnetic field (EMF) meters are utilized extensively in the subject of paranormal investigation; nevertheless, they also have practical applications in other fields. These meters are utilized in industrial settings for the purpose of evaluating electromagnetic interference, with the goal of ensuring that sensitive equipment is not adversely affected. In addition, electromagnetic field meters are utilized in the field of environmental health to evaluate the extent to which individuals are exposed to electromagnetic fields in a variety of environments. These meters are utilized in building inspections to identify potential electrical problems.

Using EMF Meters for Research on the Paranormal

Investigating the Paranormal and Engaging in Ghost Hunting:

Within the realm of paranormal research, electromagnetic field (EMF) meters have become increasingly popular, particularly in the realms of ghost hunting and paranormal investigations. The assumption that spirits, which are sometimes thought of as being constituted of energy, are able to influence or control electromagnetic fields in order to manifest their presence is the foundation of the concept that underpins the incorporation of these devices. In order to identify unusual readings that are said to be associated with the presence of ghosts or other forms of paranormal activity, ghost hunters make use of electromagnetic field (EMF) meters.

Correlation with Experiences Suggesting the Paranormal:

The links between spikes in electromagnetic field readings and alleged paranormal experiences are frequently documented by investigators of the paranormal. Among these experiences include the possibility of seeing apparitions, hearing sounds that cannot be explained, and experiencing other phenomena that are connected with ghostly encounters. Some people believe that the presence of a spirit that is attempting to manifest or communicate might be inferred from the presence of electromagnetic fluctuations that are irregular.

Ghostly Places and Electromagnetic Field Readings:

Enhanced electromagnetic field (EMF) readings are a characteristic of several supposedly haunted sites. There is a possibility that these high readings are caused by leftover energy imprints due to traumatic experiences or emotional incidents, according to some scientific theories. Researchers that study the paranormal frequently concentrate their attention on such areas, employing electromagnetic field meters (EMF meters) as one of the tools to evaluate the electromagnetic environment and its possible connection to the occurrence of paranormal phenomena.

Criticisms and Controversies Regarding

There is a degree of subjectivity involved:

In the field of paranormal research, the subjectivity of interpretation is one of the most significant concerns that surround the usage of electromagnetic field meters (EMF meters). Skeptics contend that the association between unusual electromagnetic field readings and paranormal experiences is founded on perceptions and interpretations that are based on personal experience. Because of the influence of human perception, which is influenced by expectations, beliefs, and environmental circumstances, it is possible for investigators to give significance to oscillations that have explanations that are more ordinary.

Standards that are not being met:

The lack of standardization in the application of electromagnetic field meters is another obstacle that must be overcome in the realm of paranormal research. There is no globally accepted criteria for what makes an aberrant reading, and different models, brands, and designs may yield different readings. What constitutes an anomalous reading is not a standard. The capacity to compare and replicate findings across different investigations is hindered by the lack of uniformity that exists.

Interference from a Technological and Environmental Perspective:

Electromagnetic field (EMF) meters are delicate units that are susceptible to being affected by a wide range of environmental and technical influences. There are several things that can cause interference, including power lines, electrical appliances, electronic devices, and even the equipment that the investigators themselves utilize.

Skeptics contend that, rather than being the result of paranormal activity, these factors are responsible for a significant number of the aberrant findings.

Assumption of Natural Fields That Is Not Correct:

The measurements that are obtained from electromagnetic field meters can also be influenced by natural sources of electromagnetic fields, such as geological formations or the magnetic field formed by the Earth. It is possible for investigators to incorrectly view natural oscillations as being of a supernatural character if they do not have a comprehensive understanding of the baseline electromagnetic environment.

Investigations and Studies in the Scientific Field

The Field Research:

Field studies have been carried out by a few researchers in order to study the possibility of a correlation between extraordinary electromagnetic field readings and the occurrence of paranormal encounters. In this research, electromagnetic fields are measured in areas that are rumored to be haunted, and at the same time, any alleged ghostly encounters are documented. The limits of such studies are acknowledged, and skeptics say that additional controlled study is required. Despite the fact that certain findings imply a correlation, the limitations need to be addressed.

Experiments That Are Undertakers:

An investigation of the ways in which electromagnetic fields influence human perception and experience has been developed to be carried out through controlled tests. In order to determine whether or not exposure to electromagnetic fields (EMF) has an effect on reported paranormal experiences, these experiments subject individuals to controlled EMF conditions. There is a wide range of findings from these trials, with some indicating that there may be a connection between exposure to electromagnetic fields (EMF) and altered states of consciousness.

Perspectives on Neurological Matters:

Researchers have investigated the possibility that electromagnetic fields could have an effect on the human brain and the cognitive processes that occur within it. The purpose of this line of investigation is to determine whether or whether being exposed to particular electromagnetic frequencies can cause altered states of consciousness or perceptual anomalies, which will contribute to the occurrence of ghostly encounters that have been observed. Additionally, there is a need for additional research in this field because the neuroscientific basis of these effects is complicated.

How EMF Meters Will Develop in the Future of Paranormal Research

Innovations in the Field of Technology:

There is a possibility that future editions of electromagnetic field meters will have expanded features and capabilities as technology continues to advance. For the purpose of achieving more precise and trustworthy measurements, advancements in sensor technology, data logging, and real-time analysis could be contributing factors. In addition, the combination of cutting-edge imaging technology with electromagnetic field (EMF) measurements has the potential to offer a more thorough understanding of the electromagnetic environment in the context of paranormal investigations.

Collaboration across Disciplines as follows:

The future of study into the paranormal may involve more collaboration between researchers who investigate the paranormal and scientists from a variety of fields, such as physics, psychology, and neuroscience. The study of paranormal occurrences, including the function of electromagnetic fields, could benefit from the introduction of fresh ideas and methodology if it were approached from an interdisciplinary perspective.

Protocols and Standardization:

For the purpose of establishing credibility within the scientific community, it is essential to address the lack of standards that exist in the field of paranormal research. In order to conduct research that is more rigorous and reproducible, the establishment of standardized protocols for the use of electromagnetic field meters (EMF meters), which include calibration procedures and baseline measurements, could be contributing.

Considerations that are Ethical:

Ethical considerations in paranormal research, such as the health and safety of participants and the ethical representation of the subject in the media, will continue to be of the utmost importance. When conducting paranormal investigations, researchers have a responsibility to emphasize the ethical treatment of participants, ensuring that they give their informed consent, and reducing the chance for experiencing suffering.

The use of electromagnetic field meters (EMF meters) has become an indispensable instrument in the field of paranormal research. Their applications range from ghost hunting to more comprehensive inquiries into the inexplicable. The disputes and discussions that surround the relevance of these gadgets continue to exist, despite the fact that they have caught the imagination of both enthusiasts and researchers.

Researchers and investigators are faced with a number of obstacles, including the subjectivity of interpretation, the absence of standards, and the vulnerability to contamination from the environment. However, due to the intricacy of the phenomenon, further investigation is required. Although scientific investigations and controlled tests have provided insights into the probable linkages between electromagnetic fields and reported paranormal experiences, further investigation is still required.

As the subject of paranormal research continues to progress, it is possible that the future may bring about technological breakthroughs, an increase in collaboration between students from different fields, and the creation of standardized protocols. This will ensure that the pursuit of understanding the paranormal is carried out with sensitivity, respect, and a commitment to scientific rigor.

Ethical considerations will continue to play a vital role in responsible research procedures. Those who are persistently fascinated by the unknown continue to be captivated by the pursuit of unraveling the secrets of the paranormal, with electromagnetic field meters serving as essential instruments in the investigator's inventory.

Chapter 5

Residual Hauntings: A Time-Loop in the Quantum Fabric

Paranormal enthusiasts and researchers have been fascinated by residual hauntings for a very long time. These hauntings are frequently portrayed as echoes from the past. Repetitive, non-interactive apparitions or events that appear to replay like a loop, creating the impression that they are imprinted on the environment are the defining characteristics of these occurrences. An increasing number of fringe theories propose that there is a connection between residual hauntings and the complexities of quantum physics. This is in contrast to the standard explanations, which frequently rely on psychological or spiritual aspects. Within the scope of this investigation, the idea of residual hauntings as a possible time-loop in the quantum fabric is investigated. This investigation helps to bridge the gap between the paranormal and the frontiers of scientific research.

Familiarizing Oneself with Residual Hauntings

Characteristics and Definition of the Term:

To differentiate themselves from interactive or intelligent hauntings, residual hauntings are distinguished by the fact that the entities or events involved do not interact with the living. Instead, they seem to be remnants of events that have occurred in the past, similar to a scene that occurs repeatedly. Appearances, sounds, or even smells that are connected with a historical event or emotionally intense time are examples of common manifestations.

The Resonance of the Environment:

The concept of environmental resonance is frequently cited as the explanation for residual hauntings, according to a theory that is widely accepted in traditional paranormal circles. According to this hypothesis, particular areas, particularly those that were infused with intense emotions, are able to preserve energy from events that occurred in the past. After that, the environment will replay these energies, which will result in the residual hauntings that have been documented.

Criticism and skepticism concerning:

Those who are skeptical about residual hauntings frequently reject them as nothing more than psychological phenomena, stating that ambient circumstances, suggestibility, and cognitive biases are all aspects that lead to the experience of recurrent occurrences. The recurring tales of lingering hauntings across cultures and historical periods continue to drive interest and inquiry, despite the skepticism that has been expressed.

Time, entanglement, and superposition is the subject of the quantum framework

Quantum physics refers to time as:

In quantum physics, time is a term that is both difficult to understand and difficult to pin down. In traditional Newtonian physics, time is shown as a path that is both constant and linear. However, quantum mechanics inserts a level of uncertainty and non-linearity into the equations they describe. Questions about the nature of time, such as whether it is continuous or quantized, are a source of contention among quantum physicists.

Entanglement of Quantum Objects:

Quantum entanglement is a phenomena that occurs when two or more particles become intertwined in such a way that the state of one particle instantaneously impacts the state of the other particle, regardless of the distance that separates them. Classical concepts of causality are called into question by this concept, which also hints at a level of interconnectivity that goes beyond what we can comprehend in our general comprehension.

Superposition that is Quantum:

A further fundamental principle that enables particles to exist in numerous states at the same time is known as quantum superposition. This idea is notably demonstrated by Schrodinger's cat, which is a thought experiment in which a cat that is contained within a closed box exists in a state of superposition, appearing to be both alive and dead all the time until it is observed. Through the process of observation, the superposition is reduced to a state that is completely distinct.

Residual Hauntings and the Theory of Quantum Time-Looped Systems

Within the realm of residual hauntings, quantum superposition:

Those who believe in the quantum time-loop theory claim that residual hauntings might be able to be explained by the superposition of particles that were participants in events that occurred in the past.

Within this framework, the tremendous emotional energy that is connected with a historical event has the potential to imprint itself on the quantum fabric of the environment, which can result in a superposition of states for the environment.

Environmental resonance and the phenomenon of quantum entanglement:

In order to provide an explanation for how the quantum states of particles that were involved in previous events may continue to be interconnected, quantum entanglement is invoked. This entanglement has the potential to generate a resonance in the environment, which would make it possible for the imprint of the past to endure and replicate itself under specific circumstances. After being entangled with one another, the interconnected particles continue to have an influence on one another, which is what causes the phenomenon of residual hauntings to be noticed.

Existence of a Non-Linear Time:

When it comes to quantum physics, the non-linear character of time presents a challenge to the conventional linear evolution of circumstances. The prospect of events from the past coexisting with those that are occurring in the present is made possible by the fact that quantum superposition and entanglement have the ability to impact the temporal characteristics of particles. This nonlinearity may give rise to the experience of lingering hauntings as time loops or echoes, depending on the circumstances.

Skepticism and Obstacles in the Scientific Community

Issues Concerning Quantum Measurement:

The enigmatic nature of wavefunction collapse during observation is the root cause of the issue that occurs in quantum measurement. In the event that the act of observation causes the superposition of quantum states to collapse, this raises problems regarding the manner in which the imprint of previous events can continue to exist even in the absence of constant observation. Those who are skeptical about the quantum time-loop theory claim that the quantum measurement problem poses a significant challenge to the theory.

Lack of Evidence Based on Experience:

In spite of the fact that it is intriguing, the quantum time-loop hypothesis does not have any empirical data to back up its claims. Paranormal occurrences, such as residual hauntings, are notoriously difficult to analyze and recreate in controlled environments because to their inherent complexity. Quantum explanations are held back from widespread adoption among the scientific community because there is a lack of tangible evidence to support them.

Collaboration across Disciplines as follows:

Interdisciplinary collaboration between physicists, psychologists, and paranormal investigators is required in order to bridge the gap between quantum physics and research on the paranormal. It is difficult to establish a common platform for communication and understanding because the language and methodology of each discipline are drastically different from one another when compared to one another.

The investigation of residual hauntings as possible time-loops in the quantum fabric is an intriguing junction between the realms of quantum physics and the realm of the supernatural. The quantum time-loop hypothesis presents a fresh perspective that makes an effort to reconcile the observed paranormal events with the mysterious rules of quantum mechanics. Traditional explanations frequently center their attention on spiritual or psychological components.

Skepticism and difficulties continue to be a concern, with the absence of empirical proof and the problem of quantum measurement offering substantial obstacles. In spite of this, the idea encourages conversations between researchers from other fields, such as physicists, psychologists, and paranormal investigators, which results in a novel partnership that aims to investigate the mysteries of residual hauntings.

The search to uncover the complexity of residual hauntings continues to be an exciting frontier, despite the fact that our grasp of quantum physics and the nature of time continues to improve. The exploration of the unknown continues as a testament to humanity's enduring curiosity and the ongoing pursuit of understanding the mysteries that lie beyond the veil of our current knowledge. Whether these phenomena find validation within the framework of quantum mechanics or continue to elude scientific explanation, the exploration of the unknown continues as a testament.

5.1 Understanding residual energy and its connection to haunted locations

People from all over the world have, for a very long time, been fascinated with haunted places because they are steeped in history and are frequently associated with stories of incidents that are considered to be supernatural. In the realm of paranormal occurrences, one of the most intriguing aspects is the concept of residual energy, which refers to an energy imprint that appears to remain in particular locations, hence giving rise to the phenomenon of hauntings. The purpose of this investigation is to bridge the gap between the mystical and the scientific by delving into the concept of residual energy, its potential origins, and its connection to haunted locales.

Defining the Concept of Residual Energy

Concept of Energy That Is Left Over:

In the context of paranormal occurrences, the term "residual energy" refers to the lasting energetic imprint that is left behind by events that occurred in the past or by emotionally intense feelings. It is believed that this leftover energy remains in a particular spot, and it frequently takes the form of apparitions, sounds, or other sensory experiences that appear to repeat themselves in a monotonous manner. Residual energy, on the other hand, is not interactive and appears to be recorded on a spectral tape recorder, in contrast to interactive hauntings, which allow the living to interact with the spirits of the deceased.

The Resonance of the Environment:

The concept of environmental resonance proposes that some sites have the ability to store and re-create energy from events that occurred in the past. The idea that emotional or traumatic events leave an impression on the environment, leaving a kind of energetic residue that may be sensed or experienced by individuals who are in close proximity to the event, is consistent with this concept.

Sources of Energy That Are Left Over

Distresses from the Past:

A history of horrific events, such as battles, murders, or natural disasters, is frequently the cause of haunted locales around the world. It is claimed that the emotional intensity that is involved with these events leaves an impression on the surroundings, leaving behind residual energy that can be sensed or witnessed by persons who are sensitive to phenomena of this nature.

Residue of Emotionalism:

The creation of residual energy is assumed to be influenced by intense emotions, regardless of whether such feelings are pleasant or negative. There is a possibility that places where people have experienced tremendous joy, grief, terror, or love may preserve an energetic residue connected with one of those feelings. It is possible for this residue to have an effect on the surroundings and contribute to the occurrence of hauntings.

Activities that are repetitive:

There is a possibility that over time, residual energy will accumulate in locations that have been the site of repetitive actions, such as rituals, ceremonies, or daily routines.

It's possible that the consistent patterns of energy associated with these activities could leave an impression on the environment, which would then contribute to the paranormal phenomena that have been documented in those various locales.

The Psychic Continuum:

Some hypotheses postulate the presence of psychic residue, which can be defined as the energy that remains after thoughts, intentions, or consciousness have been absorbed. In the event if people in a particular region had powerful ideas or intentions, particularly during times of crisis or emotional intensity, the psychic residue that resulted from these mental states may potentially contribute to the production of residual energy.

Creating a Connection Between Haunted Locations and Residual Energy
Repercussions on the Environment:

The idea that environmental imprints from previous events continue to exist and have an effect on the present is the foundation of the connection between residual energy and haunted locales. In the course of their investigations, paranormal investigators frequently concentrate on the past of an area, with the goal of discovering occurrences that may have left an enduring energetic imprint.

Ghostly Phenomena and Other Strange Occurrences:

It is common knowledge that apparitions and other ghostly events are typically related with residual energy in haunted areas. It is possible for witnesses to report seeing individuals or scenes that appear to be a repeat of a particular incident that occurred in the past. The apparitions in question are frequently non-interactive and give the impression of existing within their own temporal loop.

The experiences of the senses and the ears:

The presence of residual energy in haunted places may also be associated with aural experiences, such as sounds that cannot be explained, footsteps, or voices without explanation. Individuals may also report sensory experiences, such as changes in temperature, scents, or the sensation of being touched, all of which are regarded to be manifestations of leftover energy. In addition, individuals may record sensorial experiences.

Different Points of View, Scientific and Skeptical
Factors Related to Psychology:

Skeptics sometimes speculate that psychological variables, such as suggestion, expectation, and the power of belief, are responsible for the occurrence of hauntings and experiences that have been claimed in haunted locales. The sensitivity of the human mind to cognitive biases and the influence of cultural narratives can both contribute to the formation of perceptions and the interpretation of everyday occurrences as being of a supernatural nature.

Explanations Regarding the Environment:

Potential environmental causes for claimed paranormal encounters include high levels of electromagnetic fields (EMF) and infrasound, natural geological features, and even atmospheric conditions. These are all examples of environmental factors that have been taken into consideration. Skeptics contend that these elements have the potential to alter the human brain and perception, which has the potential to result in sensations or experiences that are typically associated with haunted locales.

Misinterpretation of the Energy That Is Left Over:

There are many who are opposed to the concept of residual energy and argue that many of the incidents that have been reported can be explained by a misunderstanding of natural processes or by coincidences. As an illustration, swings in temperature or drafts can result in the sense of cold areas, and sounds that cannot be explained can be produced by creaking floors or structures that are settling.

Recent Developments in the Exploration of the Paranormal

Tools related to technology:

For the purpose of documenting and measuring the possible residual energy in haunted areas, paranormal investigators are increasingly beginning to rely on technology techniques. There are a variety of technologies that are utilized in order to collect and study environmental circumstances that are connected with alleged paranormal occurrences. Some of these tools include electromagnetic field (EMF) meters, infrared cameras, and audio recording devices.

The Logging and Analysis of Data to:

Monitoring and recording environmental conditions over extended periods of time is made possible for investigators through the utilization of data logging.

The purpose of this strategy is to identify patterns and correlations between the reported encounters of the paranormal and the things that are present in the environment. In the process of discovering anomalies that may be consistent with the idea of residual energy, data analysis techniques are of great use.

Regarding the Ethical Implications of Research on the Paranormal

Participant Health and Happiness:

Investigating the paranormal requires the participation of individuals who may be sensitive to the phenomena that are being reported or who may experience distress while the inquiry is being conducted. Investigators have a responsibility to prioritize informed consent, psychological support, and respect for the experiences of those who are involved in the study. Maintaining the well-being of those who are participating in the study is an important ethical factor.

Participation in the Media That Is Responsible:

There are ethical considerations regarding appropriate representation that are raised by the portrayal of haunted locales in the media, which includes television shows and documentaries. One of the factors that can contribute to the persistence of myths and misconceptions regarding paranormal occurrences is the use of sensationalism and dramatization for the goal of entertainment.

The comprehension of residual energy and its relationship to haunted locales requires a careful balance between the scientific investigation of the paranormal and the beliefs of those who believe in the supernatural. Skeptics underline the necessity for critical analysis and evaluation of psychological and environmental factors, despite the fact that the concept is consistent with the rich tapestry of ghost stories and supernatural folklore because it does align with these elements.

As the methods of investigating the paranormal continue to develop, technological developments and improvements in data analysis contribute to a more sophisticated assessment of the hauntings that have been reported. The concept of residual energy acts as a bridge between the realms of the inexplicable and the scientific, and it is at this point that the effort to solve the secrets of haunted locales begins. The research of haunted locales and residual energy continues to be an intriguing voyage into the unknown, regardless of whether one approaches the topic with a belief in the supernatural or a skeptical eye.

5.2 Exploring the concept of time loops and their manifestation

Since the beginning of time, the idea of time loops, which refers to a phenomena in which a certain sequence of events repeats itself, has been a source of fascination for the human mind. There are significant problems regarding the nature of time, causality, and the possibilities of existence that are raised by the concept of being locked in a temporal loop, which has been depicted in works of literature, films, and scientific inquiry. The concept of time loops is investigated in depth in this investigation, which also investigates the manifestations of time loops, possible reasons for them, and the fascinating interaction between science and speculative fiction.

Specifying the Time Loops
Repeating Something in Time:

A time loop, often referred to as a temporal loop or a causal loop, is a conceptual framework that describes the occurrence of a series of events that continue to occur forever. In a scenario involving a time loop, individuals or things that are contained within the loop are subjected to the same events on several occasions, frequently without being aware of the recurrence. The normal linear view of time is challenged by this concept, which introduces the idea that certain occurrences can exist outside of the typical flow of events that occur in the past, in the present, and in the future.

With a foundation in physics:

Through the study of physics, and more specifically through the investigation of closed time-like curves, the theoretical foundations of time loops can be traced back to their origins. These curves, which were first proposed by physicists such as Kurt Godel and have since been developed further by other individuals, imply that there is the possibility of routes in spacetime that loop back on themselves. This would make it possible for time travel or closed causal loops to occur.

Expressions of Time Loops throughout the World

Exceptions to the Timing:

If time loops really exist, they might take the form of temporal anomalies, which are instances in which particular events or scenarios occur repeatedly without any apparent reason. A person may experience déjà vu, which is the sensation of having lived a moment before, or witness events that appear to be frighteningly similar. These anomalies may also involve persons who have this emotion.

The Recurrence of Occurrences:

When time loops are depicted in fictional works, they are frequently portrayed as situations in which characters find themselves reliving the same events over and over again. This repetition can range from circumstances that are quite unremarkable and banal to those that are more dramatic and life-changing.

Entanglement of Quantum Objects:

Quantum entanglement is a process in which particles become coupled over space and time. Some speculative ideas propose that the phenomena related with time loops could be linked to quantum entanglement. In the event that particles become entangled with one another, it is possible that information or events will repeat themselves in a manner similar to a loop.

Possible Explanations for the Existence of Time Loops

Timelines that are Parallel and the Multiverse:

Several other worlds or timelines, each with its own unique collection of occurrences and possibilities, are hypothesized to exist according to the multiverse hypothesis. Within the confines of this concept, time loops could emerge as a consequence of interactions between many timelines, hence causing events to ricochet or echo throughout parallel universes.

Traveling across time and wormholes:

There is a possibility that time travel or loops could be made possible by theoretical structures such as wormholes, which are fictitious tunnels in spacetime. It is possible that humans or items that traverse a wormhole could find themselves locked in a loop as they move between different temporal regions. This would occur if the wormhole were to connect many points in time.

Temporal paradoxes include:

There is a common association between time loops and temporal paradoxes, which are situations in which the events that occur within the loop produce logical problems. One of the most well-known examples is the grandfather paradox, which describes a situation in which a time traveler has the power to stop their own existence by changing happenings in the past. It's possible that the resolution of such dilemmas will require the construction of alternate universes or parallel timelines respectively.

The theory of the quantum time-loop:

In order to provide an explanation for time loops, several speculative theories take their cues from quantum mechanics.

The concept of quantum superposition, which asserts that particles can exist in numerous states at the same time, is cited to argue that particular events or information can persist in a looped state, which can have an effect on how time is perceived.

Speculative fiction and scientific research interact with one another

Inquiry and Exploration in the Scientific Field:

In scientific circles, the investigation of time loops frequently entails discussions on the nature of spacetime and theoretical physics regarding the nature of spacetime. Even though the scientific world has not been able to definitively establish or refute the existence of time loops, the theoretical frameworks and mathematical models that have been developed contribute to our overall comprehension of the structure of the universe.

A Discussion of Popular Culture and Speculative Fiction:

Speculative fiction has become increasingly reliant on time loops, which can be found in a variety of mediums, including books, movies, and television shows. Whether it is in classic works such as H.G. Wells' "The Time Machine" or in recent films such as "Groundhog Day" and "Edge of Tomorrow," the idea of temporal repetition has the ability to captivate audiences and provide a canvas for the exploration of topics such as fate, free will, and the consequences of one's choices.

Discussions on Philosophical Topics:

A further function that time loops provide is that they provide a setting for philosophical contemplations on the nature of existence and the human experience. The narratives that wrestle with the consequences of temporal repetition raise questions about determinism, the malleability of time, and the relevance of individual decisions. These questions arise because of the time repetition.

Paradoxes and Obstacles Facing Us

Paradox of the Grandfather:

One of the most major challenges that the concept of time loops faces is the grandfather paradox, which was described before. If changing the events of the past can result in logical errors, then this raises problems about the possibility of closed causal loops and the potential repercussions of time travel.

Continued coherence and consistency:

Storytellers and theorists alike face difficulties when it comes to the internal consistency and coherence of time loop storytelling. In order to keep a flow of events within the loop that is logical and realistic while still allowing for variety and evolution, it is necessary to give careful consideration to the principles that control the temporal framework.

The Application of Reasonableness:

When viewed from a scientific point of view, the application of time loops in practical settings is still considered questionable. Wormholes and closed time-like curves are examples of theoretical constructions that involve conditions and phenomena that have not been observed or proven by experimentation.

Possible Implications for Philosophy

Comparing Free Will with Determinism:

There are basic problems regarding determinism and free will that are raised by time loops. The concept of individual agency and the capacity to make significant decisions that have an effect on the trajectory of one's life is called into question when it is proposed that events are destined to repeat themselves in a loop.

Aspects of Existence to Consider:

Whether they are in a work of fiction or in philosophical thought experiments, people who find themselves trapped in a temporal loop frequently struggle with existential thoughts. Characters are prompted to examine the meaning of their acts, the connections they have, and the general purpose of their existence as a result of the series of experiences that they have.

The idea of time loops, which is a riveting combination of scientific speculation and imaginative storytelling, continues to enchant minds in a variety of fields. The investigation of temporal repetition raises significant concerns about the nature of time, causality, and the limits of human comprehension. These questions can be found in a variety of fields, ranging from theoretical physics to speculative fiction.

It is conceivable that the interaction between scientific discovery and speculative fiction will continue to inspire thought and creativity as scientific research continues to grow and theoretical frameworks continue to develop. Whether it is a topic of discussion in the sphere of philosophy, a motif in the world of literature and film, or a theoretical conundrum in the field of physics, the idea of time loops encourages us to contemplate the mysteries of existence and the ever-evolving nature of time itself.

5.3 Quantum entanglement's potential role in residual hauntings

In the field of paranormal occurrences, residual hauntings, which are characterized by the replay of particular events or energy imprints from the past, have been a subject of fascination for a very long time. A speculative idea has arisen, which proposes a connection between residual hauntings and the complex phenomena of quantum entanglement. This is in contrast to the traditional explanations, which frequently rely on psychological or spiritual elements. The mysteries of the paranormal are combined with the intricacies of quantum physics in this investigation, which investigates the possibility that quantum entanglement plays a role in residual hauntings.

Comprehending the Concept of Quantum Entanglement

Quantum entanglement's fundamental building blocks:

Quantum entanglement is a phenomenon that can be observed in quantum physics. It occurs when two or more particles become entangled in such a way that the state of one particle instantaneously impacts the state of the other particle, regardless of the distance that separates them. Traditional ideas of causation are called into question by this phenomena, which also hints at a level of interconnection that goes beyond what we can comprehend in our everyday lives.

Having an instantaneous influence and not being localized:

The non-local character of quantum entanglement implies that changes in the state of one entangled particle are instantly mirrored in the state of its entangled partner, regardless of the spatial separation between them. This is the case even if the two particles are located in different locations. As a result of this apparent breach of the speed-of-light limit, scientists have been left perplexed, and discussions have arisen over the nature of reality on the quantum level.

Superposition that is Quantum:

Another fundamental idea in quantum physics is the concept of quantum superposition, which enables particles to exist in several states at the same time. The thought experiment known as Schrodinger's cat is a well-known example of this concept. In this experiment, a cat is placed within a closed box, and until it is viewed, it exists in a state of superposition inside which it is both alive and dead. Through the process of observation, the superposition is reduced to a state that is completely distinct.

Quantum Entanglement and the Hauntings of Residual Possession

The Concept of Quantum Superposition and Temporal States

It is hypothesized by proponents of the theory that links quantum entanglement to residual hauntings that the superposition of quantum states could transcend beyond the bounds of particle physics and have an effect on the temporal states of events. Within the context of this hypothetical framework, it is possible that some occurrences or energy imprints from the past could exist in a superposition of states, which could potentially contribute to the phenomena that are observed in retained hauntings.

Information on the passage of time is entangled:

In the case that particles that were involved in events that occurred in the past become entangled, the theory suggests that the temporal information that is connected with those events could likewise become entangled. The persistence and repetition of particular temporal states could be the outcome of this entanglement, which would then lead to the phenomena that are observed in residual hauntings after they have occurred.

Transmission of Residual Energy Away from the Local Area:

The non-local transfer of information that is characteristic of quantum entanglement means that the entangled particles might influence each other immediately, even if they were separated by significant distances. When this idea is applied to residual hauntings, it is possible that the entanglement of temporal information may facilitate the transfer of residual energy over space and time, which contributes to the repeating nature of the phenomenon.

Skepticism and Obstacles in the Scientific Community

Issues Concerning Quantum Measurement:

There is an issue with quantum measurement, according to those who are opposed to the theory that emphasizes the role that quantum entanglement plays in residual hauntings. This issue presents itself as a result of the enigmatic nature of wavefunction collapse that occurs during observation. In the event that the act of observation causes the superposition of quantum states to collapse, this raises problems regarding the manner in which the imprint of previous events can continue to exist even in the absence of constant observation.

Lack of Evidence Based on Experience:

Despite the fact that it is intriguing, the theory that links quantum entanglement to residual hauntings does not currently have any empirical data to support it.

The study and replication of paranormal events, including residual hauntings, can be difficult to do in laboratories and other controlled environments. Quantum explanations are held back from widespread adoption among the scientific community because there is a lack of tangible evidence to support them.

Increasingly Complicated Quantum Phenomena:

Quantum entanglement is a phenomenon that is mostly observed at the microscopic level, and it is difficult to understand and subtle in nature. The process of extrapolating its principles to macroscopic events, particularly those that involve complicated temporal and spatial elements, presents problems and complexities that have not yet been fully understood or represented.

Possible Consequences and Prospective Prospects for the Future
Collaboration across Disciplines as follows:

The investigation of the possible role that quantum entanglement plays in residual hauntings calls for the participation of experts from a variety of fields, including cognitive scientists, physicists, and scholars who study the paranormal. For the purpose of expanding research in this speculative domain, it is vital to establish a common basis for communication and understanding amongst these various fields.

Methods of Measurement That Are More Advanced:

It is possible that developments in measurement techniques and technology will play a significant part in the investigation of the possible linkages between quantum entanglement and residual hauntings. In order to contribute to the empirical investigation of these occurrences, improved technologies that are capable of capturing and evaluating subtle energy imprints or temporal anomalies in the environment could be utilized.

The Combination of Quantum Mechanics and Studies of Consciousness:
Applications

There is a possibility that quantum phenomena and consciousness are connected, according to certain theories. Investigation into the dynamic relationship between quantum entanglement, residual hauntings, and human consciousness has the potential to yield novel understandings on the nature of paranormal experiences and the possible connections between those experiences and the perceptions of the observer.

In the realm of the research of paranormal occurrences, the investigation of the possible role that quantum entanglement plays in residual hauntings adds a dimension of complexity and mystery to the investigation.

In spite of the fact that the scientific community is skeptical of the theory because of its speculative character, it does pose some intriguing concerns about the nature of time, the interconnection of events, and the bounds of our existing understanding.

As the scientific investigation continues and technological advancements are made, the search to uncover the mysteries of residual hauntings and their possible quantum linkages may lead to new discoveries and insights. It is a monument to humanity's continuing interest and the ongoing goal of understanding the unexplained that the exploration of the unknown continues to exist, regardless of whether these occurrences find validity within the framework of quantum mechanics or remain elusive.

Chapter 6

Frequency Communication: EVP and Beyond

Over the course of many years, the investigation of supernatural occurrences has developed to incorporate a diverse range of methodology and technological approaches. EVP, or electronic voice phenomena, as well as other types of frequency communication are being investigated as part of this investigation, which is a fascinating aspect of the investigation. The term "electronic voice phenomena" (EVP) refers to the process of recording inexplicable voices or noises on electronic recording devices. This raises the possibility of a way of contact with beings that are beyond our normal perception. As part of this investigation, the historical backdrop, scientific methodologies, debates, and broader implications of frequency transmission are investigated. This investigation goes beyond the realm of extrasensory perception (EVP) to include other phenomena that are related.

Contextualization of EVP in History:

It is possible to trace the origins of Electronic Voice Phenomena all the way back to the early days of audio recording technology. The invention of the phonograph in the latter half of the 19th century made it possible to reproduce sound, which ushered in a period of time that was characterized by an obsession with recording voices that reached beyond the world of the living. During the early part of the 20th century, when radio technology was at its peak, amateur radio enthusiasts reported hearing voices and messages that were not normal appearing on their equipment. On the other hand, it wasn't until the middle of the 20th century that EVP became well known.

In 1959, the Swedish film producer and artist Friedrich Jurgenson is frequently credited with making the accidental discovery of extra-velocity particles (EVP). The voice of Jurgenson's mother, who had passed away, was allegedly heard on the cassette that he had recorded when he was out in the countryside recording bird calls. The technology that he eventually developed was called "diaphony," and it was a way in which voices were reportedly captured straight onto tape without any audible sound occurring during the recording process. He continued his research because he was intrigued by the idea.

The Latvian psychologist Konstantin Raudive worked with Jurgenson to publish his book "Breakthrough: An Amazing Experiment in Electronic Communication with the Dead" in 1971.

This book contributed to the widespread dissemination of the phenomenon of extrasensory perception (ESP). Thousands of reported recordings of extrasensory perception (EVP) were documented by Raudive, which raised the possibility that these sounds emanated from the spirit world and could be captured via the use of specialized recording techniques.

Scientific Methods for Investigating EVP:

Claims of paranormal phenomena, such as electromagnetic voice phenomena (EVP), have frequently been met with skepticism from the scientific community. The lack of controlled settings, the subjective nature of interpretation, and the possibility of contamination from environmental or technical elements are the key issues that need to be addressed. There have been attempts made by certain researchers to apply scientific procedures to the study of EVP, notwithstanding the difficulties that have been encountered.

Experiments That Are Undertakers:

The use of controlled experiments to capture EVP under standardized conditions is something that some parapsychologists and investigators of the paranormal accomplish. During these tests, recording equipment is frequently placed in supposedly haunted sites or during specific paranormal investigations. These experiments are called "paranormal investigations." In order to ensure that their conclusions are as reliable as possible, researchers strive to reduce the impact of outside factors and create an environment that is under their control.

Audio recordings are analyzed as follows:

EVP recordings are subjected to in-depth examination in order to find voices or sounds that are not typical. Software is utilized by audio engineers and researchers in order to analyze frequency patterns, remove background noise, and improve the clarity of voices that have been obtained from recordings. In order to examine EVP recordings for patterns that may not be discernible to the human ear, it is usual practice to apply spectrogram analysis, which is a method that creates a visual representation of the frequency content of sound.

Tests Conducted Without Seeing:

The use of blind testing procedures is something that some researchers perform in an effort to address concerns linked to interpretation bias and suggestion bias. When conducting blind testing, persons who are studying EVP recordings are devoid of any knowledge regarding the situations or locations related with the recordings. The purpose of this method is to reduce the level of influence that prior conceptions or expectations have on the interpretation of the sounds that have been recorded.

The Controls of the Environment:

It is common practice for researchers to employ environmental controls during EVP sessions in order to reduce the impact of external influences. The isolation of recording equipment from electrical sources, the monitoring of electromagnetic fields, and the reduction of ambient noise are all examples of controls that could fall under this category. The researchers are attempting to eliminate the possibility of conventional explanations for the sounds that are not typical by setting controlled conditions.

Discussions on Controversy and Skepticism:

In the same way that many other paranormal phenomena are met with suspicion and controversy, EVP is not that. Some people believe that the interpretation of strange sounds as voices from the spirit world is subjective and open to suggestion. But others disagree with this interpretation. The phenomenon of pareidolia, in which the human mind interprets meaningful patterns or voices in random data, is frequently offered as a possible explanation for extrasensory perception (EVP).

Additionally, detractors point out the limitations of audio recording technology, which include the fact that it is susceptible to interference from radio signals, electrical equipment, and even stray radio broadcasts. It is possible that the random nature of radio frequency interference, in conjunction with the human predisposition to discern patterns in noise, may be a contributing factor in the production of noises that are similar to EVPs but do not have a supernatural origin.

Another source of dispute is the inconsistency that can be found in EVP recordings when comparing them obtained from different sessions or places. It is reasonable to anticipate that one would obtain consistent findings under situations that are comparable if EVP were a dependable way of communication with the spirit world. Questions regarding the validity and repetition of the phenomenon are raised as a result of the fact that the quality and substance of EVP recordings do not always remain consistent.

Furthermore, the lack of a theoretical framework that explains how and why spirits or beings might interact through electrical devices presents a challenge to the scientific plausibility of extrasensory perception (EVP). Skeptics say that it is premature to attribute recorded voices to the supernatural because there is not yet a well-established model that can account for the mechanisms that are involved.

Proponents of extrasensory perception suggest that the phenomenon should be investigated further if it is done with scientific rigor and controls, despite the problems that have been presented.

In their argument, they argue that completely disregarding extrasensory perception (EVP) could be detrimental to the investigation of potentially ground-breaking discoveries in the fields of consciousness, communication, and the existence of reality.

From Extrasensory Perception to Other Phenomena and Concepts:

Even while extrasensory perception (EVP) is one of the most well-known types of frequency communication in the field of paranormal research, there are a number of phenomena and concepts that are related to it that add to a more comprehensive understanding of communication that goes beyond the human senses. The disciplines of metaphysics, consciousness research, and the investigation of the unknown are all encompassed by these phenomena.

The acronym "ITC" stands for "instrumental technology.

The phrase "instrumental transcommunication" refers to a more general concept that encompasses a variety of approaches to the utilization of electronic instruments for the purpose of communicating with entities that are outside our normal experience. EVP is not the only thing that is included in ITC; it also covers visual occurrences that are documented on video or photography equipment. Researchers assert that they have captured images, symbols, or even video recordings that they interpret as evidence of communication with non-physical entities or spirits. These researchers claim to have captured these things.

In addition to Ghost Boxes, Spirit Boxes:

A continuous stream of white noise is produced by electrical devices known as spirit boxes, which are also referred to as ghost boxes. These devices scan across radio frequencies at a tremendous rate. These gadgets are utilized by paranormal investigators who are under the impression that spirits are able to modify audio fragments in order to communicate with them. In order to correctly understand the responses that are received from spirit boxes, it is frequently necessary to recognize pertinent words or phrases within the random noise.

In the realm of radio frequency identification (RFID) and communication with the paranormal:

There are researchers that investigate the paranormal who are looking into the possibility of using RFID technology to communicate with entities. It is hypothesized that in order to communicate with one another, ghosts or other entities might be able to manipulate RFID signals or devices. This idea extends to the investigation of techniques that could make it easier for people to communicate between the physical and metaphysical realms through the use of advanced technology.

Communication that are responsive to thought:

It is hypothesized under the thought-responsive communication theory that consciousness itself might be involved in the occurrence of many paranormal occurrences. There is a school of thinking among researchers that suggests entities might be able to interact directly with individuals through their thoughts, so avoiding the use of traditional methods such as audio or visual signals. This idea is consistent with more general hypotheses concerning the nature of consciousness and the ways in which it may interact with the outside environment.

"The Global Consciousness Project," often known as "GCP"

Roger Nelson, a professor at Princeton University, is the one who founded the worldwide Consciousness Project, which investigates the possibility of a relationship between human consciousness and significant events on a worldwide scale. For the purpose of determining whether or not patterns emerge during big global events, the project makes use of random number generators that are dispersed across the globe. The GCP raises questions regarding the role of consciousness in influencing and maybe surpassing traditional systems of communication, despite the fact that it is not directly related to extraordinary visual perception (EVP).

Progress in the Fields of Science and Technology:
New pathways for the investigation of frequency communication and other paranormal events have been made available as a result of developments in scientific instruments and technology. At this point in time, researchers have access to advanced equipment that enables them to gather, analyze, and interpret data with greater precision. The incorporation of technology into investigations of the paranormal has resulted in an increase in the level of exploration as well as the birth of new problems for those conducting the investigations.

Audio recording in digital format:
As a result of the move from analog to digital audio recording, the quality and clarity of the sounds that have been recorded have been substantially enhanced. Digital recording makes it possible to conduct a more in-depth examination of frequency patterns, which in turn lessens the influence of background noise and makes it easier for researchers to identify probable executive voice phenomena (EVP). On the other hand, the digital format has also brought about new difficulties, such as the alteration of recordings through the use of editing software.

System Software for Spectral Analysis:
When it comes to the inspection of audio recordings for the presence of unusual frequencies, spectral analysis software has emerged as a very useful instrument.

Researchers have the ability to view and analyze the frequency content of recorded sounds with the use of this program, which ultimately assists in the identification of patterns or voices that may not be immediately evident. The scientific rigor that is given to the investigation of EVP is improved with the utilization of spectral analysis.

Equipment for Monitoring in Real Time:
For the purpose of conducting investigations into the paranormal, real-time monitoring systems that offer instant feedback are now being utilized by investigators. Some examples of these equipment are audio spectrum analyzers, which are capable of displaying frequency patterns in real time, as well as devices that are able to translate oscillations in electromagnetic fields into sounds that can be heard. Researchers are able to respond to reported phenomena as they occur when they are monitored in real time, which strengthens the participatory and dynamic aspect of paranormal investigations.

Experiments that are Structured and Include Control Groups:
Some researchers undertake organized studies with control groups in an effort to address criticisms that are related to the absence of controlled conditions in investigations of the paranormal. These studies are designed to produce controlled conditions for the gathering of data, as well as to isolate variables, eliminate potential sources of contamination, and eliminate potential sources of contamination. Researchers are attempting to bolster the legitimacy of their conclusions by incorporating scientific procedures into their work.

Considerations of Ethical Implications and Obstacles:
There are inherent obstacles and ethical considerations that researchers and

investigators must take into account when conducting research on frequency communication, which includes the investigation of EVP and other related occurrences. It is essential to address these problems in order to preserve the credibility of paranormal research and to cultivate an approach that is responsible and respectful toward the unknown.

In terms of interpretation and subjectivity:

Considering that the interpretation of EVP recordings is always subjective, there are issues that arise in relation to confirmation bias and expectation. It's possible that researchers and investigators will interpret noises in a way that is consistent with their own opinions or preconceived conceptions; this could happen by accident. It is difficult to differentiate between genuine paranormal events and artifacts or random noise that could be misunderstood as communication. This is the challenge.

Consistency and the ability to reproduce:

There is a lack of consistency in the recordings of EVPs between multiple sessions, locations, or investigators, which raises issues regarding the dependability and replicability of the phenomenon. The establishment of uniform techniques and defined protocols for EVP research is absolutely necessary in order to construct a foundation of evidence that can be relied upon. A significant factor that helps to the credibility of the findings is the replication of the results under controlled conditions.

Treatment of Entities in an Ethical Manner:

When researchers have the confidence that they are conversing with beings or spirits, there are ethical considerations that must be taken into account regarding how these entities should be treated. With the presumption that there are intelligent entities engaged, researchers are required to approach their job with respect and empathy, taking into consideration the potential consequences that their actions may have on the entities that are involved. When developing ethical rules, it is important to give priority to the health and independence of any non-physical entities that may be acting as participants in communication.

Technology Utilization That Is Responsible:

As technology continues to play an important part in investigations into the paranormal, it is of the utmost importance that this technology be used in a responsible manner. By virtue of the fact that there is a possibility of technological artifacts, false positives, or manipulation of recordings, there is a requirement for ethical rules to be implemented when using electronic devices. Researchers must make transparency in their procedures a top priority, freely reporting the technology that they use and any post-processing that is applied to recordings from the beginning.

Impact on Those Who Believe and Those Who Took Part:

It is possible for believers and participants to have tremendous emotional and psychological impacts as a result of the transmission of EVP recordings, particularly those recordings that are interpreted as communication with the deceased person. When doing research, it is important for researchers to be aware of the potential impact their findings could have on those who are experiencing grief or who are looking for comfort through the possibility of communicating with loved ones. When it comes to the responsible sharing and interpretation of evidence obtained through electronic voice recording (EVP), ethical considerations should be extended.

There is a fascinating convergence of technology, consciousness, and the unknown that is represented by the investigation of frequency transmission, which is exhibited by phenomena such as Electronic Voice Phenomena (EVP).

The concept of frequency communication continues to captivate the imaginations of researchers, paranormal enthusiasts, and the general public. Its historical roots may be traced back to early audio recording studies, and it is currently being investigated with advanced gear.

From the earliest tests with audio recording technology to the popular interest in capturing voices from the afterlife, the historical backdrop of extraterrestrial voice phenomena (EVP) demonstrates a trend. Friedrich Jurgenson and Konstantin Raudive were among the pioneers who played a significant part in the process of popularizing extrasensory perception (EVP) and establishing it as a subject of study within the metaphysical community.

Scientific methods to extrasensory perception (EVP) have attempted to apply rigorous methodologies to the investigation of anomalous auditory occurrences, despite the fact that obstacles linked to subjectivity and interpretation have been encountered. Experimental methods such as controlled studies, blind testing, and advanced analysis techniques are all contributing factors in the continued search for empirical evidence of communication that goes beyond the typical.

In the scientific and paranormal worlds, the necessity for critical scrutiny and open discourse is brought to light by the controversies and skepticism that surround extrasensory psychophysical phenomena (EVP). There are a number of obstacles that stand in the way of widespread acceptance of electronic voice phenomena (EVP) as a legitimate method of communication with the supernatural. These include the limitations of audio recording technology, the possibility of contamination, and the lack of a clearly defined theoretical framework.

The investigation of related phenomena, such as instrumental transcommunication (ITC), spirit boxes, and RFID technology, broadens the area of frequency communication study. This is in addition to the investigation of extra-velocity phenomena (EVP). Thought-responsive communication and the Global Consciousness Project are two examples of concepts that provide new pathways for exploring the potential interaction between consciousness and the paranormal.

Scientific and technological breakthroughs, such as digital audio recording, spectrum analysis software, real-time monitoring devices, and structured experiments, all contribute to the refining of research procedures for the study of the paranormal. Researchers are provided with more precise means of investigating the unknown as a result of these instruments, which improve the quality of data gathering, processing, and interpretation.

There are a number of challenges and ethical issues that highlight the significance of taking a thoughtful and ethical approach to frequency communication research. Some of these challenges include subjectivity in interpretation, consistency in results, responsible use of technology, and considerations regarding the influence on believers and participants. It is vital to strike a balance between scientific rigor and empathy and respect for the entities, regardless of whether they are seen as spiritual beings or expressions of awareness, in order to cultivate an inquiry of the paranormal that is both responsible and inclusive.

In spite of the fact that the subject of paranormal research is constantly undergoing development, frequency communication continues to be an intriguing frontier that calls for additional investigation. Whether viewed through the lens of scientific inquiry, metaphysical exploration, or a combination of the two, the study of extrasensory perception (ESP) and related phenomena contributes to our continual quest to grasp the mysteries that lay beyond the bounds of our conventional senses.

6.1 Analyzing Electronic Voice Phenomena (EVP) through a scientific lens

The phenomenon known as electronic voice phenomena (EVP) is a fascinating and mysterious part of paranormal investigation that invites both curiosity and skepticism. There is a phenomenon that involves the claimed recording of voices or noises that cannot be explained on electrical recording devices. This occurrence suggests that there may be a type of contact with things that exist outside the world of conventional perception. In spite of the fact that extrasensory perception (EVP) has been a topic of fascination for paranormal investigators and aficionados, analyzing it via a scientific lens necessitates a comprehensive assessment of methodology, problems, and the broader implications for our comprehension of consciousness and the nature of reality.

Methodologies utilized in the scientific evaluation of EVP:

When it comes to the investigation of Electronic Voice Phenomena, applying scientific principles requires taking a methodical approach to the collecting of data, the conduct of experiments, and the interpretation of the results. Researchers make an effort to adhere to scientific techniques in order to boost the legitimacy and reliability of their findings, despite the fact that EVP research occurs inside the realm of the paranormal.

Experiments That Are Under Control The use of controlled experiments is one of the most important aspects of the scientific investigation of EVPs. For the purpose of capturing EVP within predetermined boundaries, these studies include the establishment of particular conditions, which are typically carried out in supposedly haunted locales or during investigations into the paranormal.

Through the establishment of controlled conditions, researchers intend to reduce the impact of external factors and enhance the possibility of capturing abnormal auditory occurrences.

Utilization of Digital Audio Recording: The movement away from analog audio recording technology and towards digital audio recording technology has had a significant impact on EVP analysis. The use of digital recording makes it possible to create recordings that are more distinct and of greater quality, which in turn enables researchers to more efficiently catch and analyze small noises. In addition, the utilization of digital technology makes it easier to implement sophisticated audio analysis methods, which contributes to the scientific rigor of EVP study.

Software for Spectral Analysis: In recent years, spectral analysis software has emerged as an indispensable source of information for the scientific investigation of EVP recordings. It is possible for researchers to display and analyze the frequency content of recorded sounds in great detail with the help of this program. Researchers have the ability to uncover abnormalities that may suggest the presence of voices or noises that are not apparent to the human ear by analyzing frequency patterns. The process of analysis is made more precise and objective by the utilization of spectral analysis methodology.

In order to address issues regarding suggestion and interpretation bias, researchers frequently incorporate blind testing procedures into their studies. When conducting blind testing, persons who are studying EVP recordings are devoid of any knowledge regarding the situations or locations related with the recordings. This method helps to reduce the influence of any preconceived beliefs or expectations that may have been present during the interpretation of the recorded sounds, which ultimately results in a more objective analysis.

Environmental Controls: Environmental controls are an essential component of scientific EVP analysis because of the possibility that recordings of EVP events could be influenced by things that are external to the recording. In order to limit ambient noise, researchers use steps to monitor electromagnetic fields, isolate recording equipment from electrical sources, and monitor electromagnetic fields. Researchers are attempting to exclude the possibility of traditional explanations for aberrant noises, such as interference or contamination, by setting controlled conditions.

Replication of Results: The ability to reproduce results is an essential component of scientific investigation. The objective of the researchers is to duplicate the results of the EVP under situations that are comparable in order to evaluate the consistency and reliability of the phenomena. One factor that adds to the reliability of EVP findings is the capability of reproducing sounds that are not typical in a variety of sessions or settings.

In addition, replication makes it possible to recognize patterns and trends that may arise as a result of several studies being conducted.

Obstacles Facing the Scientific Examination of EVPs:

In spite of the fact that scientific approaches are utilized, EVP analysis is confronted with a number of obstacles that call for a nuanced and analytical approach. In order to preserve the integrity of the scientific community and make progress in our understanding of the phenomenon, it is essential that these problems be addressed:

Subjectivity and Interpretation: The subjective nature of interpretation is one of the key obstacles that arises while conducting an EVP study. The human mind is susceptible to the phenomena known as pareidolia, which occurs when significant patterns, such as voices, are seen in inputs that are completely random. Researchers are forced to contend with the possibility of subjective interpretation, particularly when they are seeking to decipher words or messages from sounds that are unclear or obscure.

The potential for contamination exists in the fact that electronic voice recording (EVP) recordings are susceptible to contamination from a variety of sources, such as radio signals, electronic gadgets, and stray radio broadcasts. It is possible that the random nature of radio frequency interference, in conjunction with the human predisposition to discern patterns in noise, may be a contributing factor in the production of noises that are similar to EVPs but do not have a supernatural origin. It is necessary to conduct comprehensive study and take into consideration the various potential causes of interference in order to differentiate between genuine EVP and contaminating variables.

The absence of established procedures and protocols in EVP research presents issues for maintaining consistency and comparing different studies. This is because of the lack of standardization. When it comes to establishing uniform criteria for EVP analysis, it is difficult to do so because different researchers and paranormal investigators use a wide variety of methodologies and methods. The process of standardization is absolutely necessary in order to establish a strong basis for scientific investigation into the phenomenon.

EVP analysis does not have a well-defined theoretical framework that explains how and why entities might communicate through electronic devices. This is a limitation of the framework. The lack of a comprehensive model is a barrier to the scientific plausibility of extrasensory perception (EVP). Researchers confront difficulties in establishing hypotheses and predictions that can lead to rigorous investigation when they do not have a good knowledge of the systems that are involved.

The inclusion of human operators and participants in EVP sessions introduces a possible source of bias into the process. This is referred to as the human factor. There is a possibility that the interpretation of recorded sounds will be impacted by the expectations, beliefs, and feelings of the individuals who participated in the session. Researchers have a responsibility to be aware of the human factor and the potentially significant impact it can have on the results of EVP experiments.

Perspectives and Implications That Are More General:

When seen through the perspective of science, the investigation of Electronic Voice Phenomena not only tackles the particulars of EVP research, but it also raises more general problems concerning consciousness, perception, and the nature of reality. There is a possibility that the scientific community may approach extrasensory perception (EVP) with suspicion; nonetheless, recognizing its existence and investigating it using rigorous approaches could have substantial implications:

Consciousness and Communication: If extrasensory perception (EVP) were to be validated by scientific research, it would pose a challenge to the paradigms that now encompass consciousness and communication. The concept that beings or consciousnesses that are beyond our normal perception are able to influence electrical devices in order to deliver messages suggests that there is a level of contact that goes beyond the conventional understandings of communication.

A reassessment of the nature of reality might be prompted by the existence of extrasensory perception (EVP), provided that it is supported by scientific evidence. It is possible that the traditional borders that separate the physical and non-physical domains may become less distinct, which will challenge the preconceived beliefs that we have regarding what is feasible within the confines of our comprehension. New inquiry into the connectivity of consciousness and the fabric of reality might be prompted as a result of this.

Technological Interface with the Paranormal: The convergence of technology and the paranormal, as shown by research on extrasensory perception (EVP), presents intriguing issues concerning the potential interface between electronic equipment and non-physical entities. In the event that entities are able to communicate through electronic means, this indicates the presence of a bridge between the material and immaterial realms, which is facilitated by technology for communication.

Increasing the Boundaries of Scientific Investigation The scientific investigation of extrasensory perception (EVP) may be seen as a sign of a readiness to investigate unorthodox phenomena within the sphere of scientific research.

Recognizing the presence of anomalous auditory phenomena supports a more comprehensive approach to the study of the unknown, which in turn expands the horizons of scientific investigation beyond the bounds that have traditionally been established.

When viewed through the lens of science, the investigation of Electronic Voice Phenomena represents a dynamic junction of technology, consciousness studies, and the investigation of the supernatural. The application of scientific procedures to EVP research highlights a commitment to systematic investigation and a desire to comprehend the mysteries that lay beyond ordinary awareness. This is despite the fact that obstacles and skepticism continue to exist.

A number of factors contribute to the scientific rigor that is employed in EVP analysis. These factors include controlled experiments, digital recording equipment, spectrum analysis tools, and environmental controls. In an effort to make progress in our comprehension of this puzzling phenomenon, researchers must overcome the obstacles of subjectivity, the possibility of contamination, and the absence of standardization.

The broader ramifications of acknowledging and researching communication beyond the regular senses demand a reassessment of fundamental features of consciousness, reality, and the interface between the physical and non-physical realms. Furthermore, the specifics of extrasensory perception (EVP) research are not the only thing that is being investigated. As technology continues to play a prominent part in investigations of the paranormal, the scientific community is struggling to come to terms with the possibility of electronic gadgets and the enigmatic worlds that exist beyond our everyday experiences converging.

It is necessary to maintain a delicate balance between scientific scrutiny and open-minded inquiry as the investigation of electronic voice phenomena continues to develop. The study of extrasensory perception (EVP) is a monument to the everlasting human ambition to discover the unknown and to push the boundaries of what is deemed feasible within the vast and intricate tapestry of existence.

6.2 The physics of sound waves and their interaction with spectral frequencies

In the fields of acoustics and wave physics, one of the most fundamental aspects is the study of sound waves and how they interact with spectrum frequencies. It is possible to gain an understanding of the behavior of sound by applying the concepts of wave mechanics. Sound is a mechanical wave that travels through a variety of different media. The fundamental aspects of sound waves, the anatomy of a wave, and the interaction of sound with spectrum frequencies are all investigated in this investigation, which digs into the physics of sound waves. For a comprehensive understanding of the creation, propagation, and perception of sound in a variety of settings, it is vital to have a firm grasp on these fundamental principles.

Sound waves have the following fundamental properties:

Sound is a longitudinal wave, which means that it involves the vibration of particles along the direction that waves propagate. This is the nature of sound. Comparatively, sound waves are composed of compressions and rarefactions, in which air particles travel in a path that is parallel to the direction of the wave. This is in contrast to transverse waves, in which particles move in a direction that is perpendicular to the direction of the wave.

Both frequency and pitch are characterized by the fact that the frequency of a sound wave is measured in Hertz (Hz) and corresponds to the number of oscillations or cycles that occur in a given amount of time. The perceived pitch of a sound is determined by its frequency, with higher frequencies being thought to be connected with higher pitches and lower frequencies being thought to be related with lower pitches. The range of frequencies that humans are able to perceive is typically between 20 and 20,000 hertz.

Amplitude and Loudness: Amplitude is the maximum displacement of particles from their equilibrium position during one full cycle of a wave. Loudness is the amount of sound that is produced by a wave. Because it is a measurement of the energy that is carried by the wave, it is the factor that influences how loud a sound is perceived to be. An increase in amplitude is associated with a louder sound, whilst a decrease in amplitude is associated with a more diminished sound.

A sound wave's wavelength is the distance between two successive points that are in phase with one another. For example, two compressions or two rarefactions can be considered to be in phase with one another. The relationship between frequency and wavelength is inversely proportional, which means that waves with higher frequencies occupy shorter wavelengths and vice versa.

Characteristics of a Sound Wave:

Sound waves are made up of alternating zones of compression and rarefaction, which are referred to as compression and rarefaction, respectively. Compression is a process in which air particles are squeezed together in close proximity, which results in an increase in pressure. Rarefaction is characterized by a decrease in pressure as a result of the particles becoming more dispersed. A single complete cycle of the sound wave comprises the compression and rarefaction portions.

It is necessary for sound to go through a medium in order for it to be transmitted. Examples of such mediums are air, water, and solids. The sound source vibrates, which causes the air particles to be compressed and rarefied. This results in the formation of a pressure wave that travels through the medium. This type of wave is known as a compressional wave. The wave is caused to propagate as a result of the energy that is transmitted from the source of vibration to the particles that are within its vicinity.

The qualities of the medium through which sound travels have an effect on the speed of sound, which is described in more detail below. Approximately 343 meters per second (m/s) is the speed at which sound travels through air when it is at normal temperature. There are a number of elements that can affect the speed, including temperature, humidity, and the specific composition of the medium. Generally speaking, sound travels more quickly through a denser medium, such as water or solids, than it does through air.

The Interaction with Spectral Frequencies Includes:

A complex sound wave is broken down into its component frequencies in order to do spectral analysis, which is a type of sound analysis. The representation that is produced as a result is referred to as a frequency spectrum, and each peak corresponds to a particular frequency component. For the purpose of comprehending the construction of complex sounds, such as musical notes or spoken words, spectral analysis is an essential field of study.

Harmonics and Overtones: The existence of harmonics and overtones is another characteristic that distinguishes complex sounds, particularly those that are created by musical instruments or the human voice. On the other hand, overtones are frequencies that are higher than the fundamental frequency, whereas harmonics are integer multiples of the fundamental frequency. The distinctive timbre or quality of a sound is a result of the interaction of the fundamental frequency, harmonics, and overtones in the sound.

Natural Frequencies and Resonance: Resonance is the phenomenon that takes place when an object is subjected to a periodic force that corresponds to its natural frequency.

When it comes to sound, resonance is a phenomenon that amplifies certain frequencies, which ultimately results in an increase in amplitude. For instance, musical instruments make use of resonance to enhance particular frequencies, which results in the production of sounds that are unique and full of depth. In engineering and design, having a solid understanding of the inherent frequencies of objects is absolutely necessary.

The Fourier transform is a mathematical method that is utilized for the purpose of analyzing the frequency content of a signal, which includes sound waves. Frequency components are also a part of the Fourier transform. Through the process of decomposing a complicated waveform into its component frequencies, it is possible to determine the amplitude and phase of each frequency component. Numerous industries, ranging from the production of music to the realm of telecommunications, make extensive use of Fourier analysis.

Pitch Perception: The frequency of a sound wave is directly related to the human auditory processing that is responsible for the perception of pitch. In a situation where the frequency is increasing, the pitch is perceived as being higher, and when the frequency is decreasing, the pitch is regarded as being lower. In humans, the ability to perceive and differentiate between different pitches across a broad frequency range is made possible by the complex brain processing that occurs in the auditory system.

Implications for Technology and Applications: Technologies

Understanding the physics of sound waves and how they interact with spectrum frequencies is essential to the process of producing and synthesizing music. Knowledge of these concepts is essential. The manipulation of frequencies by musicians and audio engineers allows for the creation of a wide variety of timbres, harmonies, and textures. Both analog and digital synthesizers are dependent on the fundamentals of sound wave creation and manipulation in order to function properly.

Processing Speech and Communication Speech signals are complicated and involve a wide variety of frequencies. Speech signals are difficult to process. When it comes to speech processing and communication systems, studying the spectrum components of speech is beneficial for tasks such as voice recognition and compression. Spectral analysis is utilized by technologies such as speech recognition software in order to recognize and interpret spoken words.

Medical Imaging and Ultrasonography: The laws of sound wave propagation are the foundation upon which ultrasound technology is built in the realm of medicine. The process of creating images of internal structures in the body through the use of high-frequency sound waves is known as ultrasonography.

Medical experts are able to view organs, tissues, and anomalies in a non-invasive manner by examining the reflections of sound waves by using this technique.

Environmental Noise Environmental noise analysis is the process of evaluating and reducing the negative effects that noise has on both human health and the environment. In order to build efficient solutions for noise reduction, it is helpful to have an understanding of the frequency content of the sources of noise. Spectral analysis is utilized by technologies for noise monitoring and control in order to identify and define the many types of ambient noise.

Signal Processing and Telecommunications: In the field of telecommunications, the transmission and processing of audio signals both include the modulation of spectral frequencies. In order to send and receive information in an effective manner, signal processing techniques such as filtering and modulation are utilized. Effective communication is made possible through the utilization of these principles by technologies such as mobile phones and audio streaming services.

Sound Wave Analysis: Obstacles to Overcome and Recent Developments

The issue of distinguishing between desired signals and unwanted noise calls for the application of sophisticated signal processing techniques. Noise reduction and signal processing are two types of signal processing. In the presence of background noise, the objective of noise reduction methods like adaptive filtering and spectral subtraction is to improve the clarity of the signals that are wanted. Research that is now being conducted is centered on enhancing the effectiveness of these algorithms in a variety of settings.

Psychoacoustics and Human Perception: The study of sound perception through the lens of psychoacoustics investigates both the psychological and physiological elements of sound perception. In order to develop audio systems that are compatible with human hearing capabilities, it is helpful to have an understanding of how humans perceive and interpret sound waves, especially the spectrum components of those waves. The creation of immersive audio experiences is influenced by the progress that has been made in psychoacoustics.

Non-Destructive Testing and substance Characterization: In non-destructive testing, sound waves are utilized to evaluate the integrity and qualities of materials without causing any damage to the substance being tested. Ultrasonic testing is one example of a technique that involves analyzing the reflection and transmission of sound waves through materials in order to identify flaws or discrepancies. The resolution and accuracy of these testing procedures are the objectives of ongoing research that is now being conducted.

Audio Ecology and Urban Planning: The field of research known as acoustic ecology investigates the connection that exists between sound, the surrounding environment, and the human experience. By gaining an understanding of the spectrum features of environmental sounds, urban planners are able to develop methods that will result in the creation of urban places that are both acoustically pleasing and sustainable. New developments in acoustic ecology have made it possible to create cities that put an emphasis on both the utility and the auditory well-being of their inhabitants.

The physics of sound waves and the way in which they interact with spectral frequencies constitute a multidimensional field that has applications in a wide variety of fields, including music and communication, medical imaging, and environmental study. It is through the interaction of frequency, amplitude, and wave propagation that sound, which is a wave phenomenon, reveals its complexity. By analyzing the spectrum components of sound waves, one can gain significant insights into the composition, quality, and characteristics of a wide variety of sounds.

The laws that regulate the behavior of sound waves have far-reaching effects, ranging from the harmonics of a musical instrument to the resonance frequencies of structural elements. Continuing to use our understanding of sound wave physics for the development of creative applications, technological breakthroughs in signal processing, medical imaging, and telecommunications continue to make use of existing knowledge. The continual research that is being conducted to develop and increase our skills in sound wave analysis is being driven by the fact that challenges continue to exist in areas like noise reduction, psychoacoustics, and non-destructive testing sectors.

As we explore more into the complexities of sound wave physics, the multidisciplinary nature of this field becomes more and more apparent. By combining the fields of physics, engineering, biology, and psychology, we are able to investigate not only the fundamental aspects of sound but also the tremendous impact that sound has on our perception, communication, and the built environment. The physics of sound waves, with its intricate web of frequencies and interactions, continues to be a frontier that is always developing, which invites further investigation and discovery.

6.3 Advancements in technology for capturing and analyzing ghostly communications

A substantial amount of technological progress has been made over the course of time in the field of investigating paranormal occurrences, which includes the investigation of ghostly communications. New instruments are being utilized by researchers and individuals who are interested in the paranormal in order to record and examine potential evidence of interactions with the spirit world as technology continues to advance. The purpose of this article is to investigate some of the significant technological improvements that have been made in the field of recording and interpreting ghostly communications. The essay places an emphasis on the junction of the paranormal with the most recent scientific and technological advancements.

Audio recording in digital format: The shift from analog to digital audio recording is a significant step forward in the process of capturing phantom communications. When compared to their analog counterparts, digital audio recorders have additional storage space, higher signal-to-noise ratios, and higher quality than their analog counterparts. Through the use of this technology, investigators are able to capture faint noises and voices with more clarity, which enables them to conduct more extensive analysis during the post-processing stage.

Software for Spectral Analysis: Spectral analysis software has emerged as an indispensable instrument for paranormal investigators who are investigating electronic voice phenomena (EVP) and other forms of ghostly contact. Through the use of this software, it is possible to visualize and analyze the frequency patterns that are present in audio recordings. Through the use of spectral analysis, investigators are able to recognize abnormalities, isolate probable EVP, and differentiate them from background noise. An increase in the scientific rigor that is given to the investigation of ghostly communications is brought about by the visual display of frequency content.

Real-Time Monitoring equipment: Recent developments in real-time monitoring equipment have made it possible to conduct interactive and dynamic research surrounding the paranormal. Audio spectrum analyzers are included in these devices. These analyzers display frequency patterns in real time, which enables investigators to examine changes as they occur. Researchers are able to respond quickly to seen occurrences and capture potential spirit messages in the present when they use real-time monitoring, which amplifies the immediacy of paranormal investigations.

Both Ghost Boxes and Spirit Boxes Ghost boxes, which are also referred to as spirit boxes, are electronic devices that are meant to scan over radio frequencies in a short amount of time. These gadgets are utilized by paranormal investigators who are under the impression that spirits are able to modify audio fragments in order to communicate with them.

A constant stream of randomized audio is provided to consumers by modern ghost boxes, which are equipped with sweeping algorithms and noise reduction capabilities. There are also certain devices that come with built-in word banks, which supposedly enable spirits to choose suitable words in order to compose intelligible communications.

EVP Analysis Software: Unlike common audio editing tools, specialized EVP analysis software goes beyond the capabilities of these tools and offers features that are specifically designed for paranormal investigation. The noise reduction techniques, frequency filters, and voice recognition features that are often included in these tools are included. EVP analysis software is utilized by researchers in order to improve the clarity of recorded voices, extract probable EVP, and apply a variety of filters in order to differentiate between real paranormal noises and those that are caused by environmental or electrical interference.

Monitoring Equipment for the Environment The capabilities of environmental monitoring equipment that is utilized in paranormal investigations have been improved by technological advancements. These instruments detect a variety of variables, including temperature, electromagnetic fields (EMF), and barometric pressure, among others. There are researchers that are interested in the paranormal who feel that alterations in certain environmental factors might be associated with the existence of ghosts. By utilizing sophisticated sensors and data logging capabilities, investigators are able to collect and examine environmental data over extended periods of time, with the goal of identifying trends or anomalies that are related with ghostly activity.

Augmented Reality (AR) and Virtual Reality (VR): Technologies that utilize augmented reality and virtual reality are rapidly being applied in the field of paranormal investigations in order to create immersive experiences. Users are able to virtually experience and engage with simulated worlds or entities through the utilization of these technologies. It is possible to use augmented reality and virtual reality in the context of ghostly communications to recreate historical settings. This will make it easier for individuals to have potential interactions with ghosts or creatures that are thought to inhabit particular areas.

Machine Learning and Pattern Recognition: The application of machine learning and pattern recognition algorithms to ghostly communications marks a new frontier in the field of study on the paranormal. The use of artificial intelligence to analyze massive datasets of audio recordings is something that researchers are starting to investigate. The use of machine learning algorithms has the ability to learn to recognize patterns that are connected with paranormal events. This could be of assistance in the identification of real ghostly communications and the differentiation of these messages from conventional sounds.

It is crucial to approach research on the paranormal with a critical mentality, despite the fact that these technical breakthroughs offer intriguing prospects for recording and studying communications from ghosts. The fact that the interpretation of evidence is inherently subjective, in conjunction with the constraints imposed by the technology that is now available, highlights the importance of maintaining scientific investigation and maintaining open dialogue within the paranormal community. It is inevitable that the techniques and instruments that are utilized to investigate the mysteries of ghostly communications and the wider domain of the supernatural will continue to develop alongside the progression of technology.

Chapter 7

Interdimensional Physics: Bridging the Gap Between Realms

Within the sphere of scientific investigation, the investigation of interdimensional physics is a frontier that is both exciting and speculative. In this area of study, the potential of parallel worlds, alternate dimensions, and the presence of realities that are beyond our ordinary knowledge is investigated. In spite of the fact that it is solidly anchored in theoretical physics, the concept of interdimensional physics poses a challenge to conventional ideas regarding space, time, and the underlying fabric of the universe. The purpose of this in-depth investigation is to disentangle the intricacies of interdimensional physics by investigating theoretical frameworks, experimental concerns, and the potential ramifications for our comprehension of the world around us.

A Foundational Approach to Theory:

String Theory and Extra Dimensions: String theory, a significant theoretical framework in current physics, proposes that the fundamental building blocks of the cosmos are not point-like particles but rather small, vibrating strings. This theory provides an explanation for the existence of extra dimensions. The framework of string theory is used to postulate the existence of additional spatial dimensions in addition to the three dimensions that are commonly known (length, breadth, and height). These additional dimensions, which are frequently condensed and incomprehensible at human scales, offer a mathematical framework that can be utilized to investigate the possibility of the existence of alternative realms.

There are multiple universes, each with its own set of physical rules and constants, according to the multiverse theory, which proposes that there are multiple universes. Several different interpretations of quantum physics and the notion of cosmic inflation have led to the development of this concept. According to the theory of the multiverse, our universe is merely one of an infinite number of alternative universes that could live in parallel with one another or branch off from one another. It is possible that a great number of realities could emerge as a result of the various conditions and characteristics of these universes.

Brane Theory and Parallel Worlds: Brane theory, which is an extension of string theory, presents the concept of multidimensional structures that are referred to as "branes." Our universe, also known as a "brane," has the potential to cohabit with other branes found in a realm with higher dimensions. It is possible that interactions between these branes could have an effect on cosmic processes and could potentially give rise to effects that can be observed.

The realization of this idea paves the way for the possibility of parallel worlds existing on different brains.

Quantum Entanglement and Non-Locality: Quantum entanglement, which is a phenomena in which particles become coupled in such a way that the state of one instantaneously changes the state of the other, poses a challenge to our traditional understanding of the concept of locality. The information that is passed back and forth during entanglement may be able to transcend space time as we know it, according to certain interpretations, which offers a clue at the possibility of links across different dimensions or realms.

Wormholes and Spatial Shortcuts: Theoretical constructs that are referred to as wormholes propose the presence of shortcuts through spacetime, which may potentially connect distant areas or even separate worlds. The concept of wormholes provides a look into the possibility of traveling through the fabric of spacetime and reaching other dimensions, despite the fact that it is open to speculation and necessitates the existence of unusual forms of matter in order to maintain stability.

Considerations Regarding the Experiment:

Particle Accelerators and Extra Dimensions: High-energy particle accelerators are being used in the experimental investigations that are being conducted to investigate the meaning of extra dimensions. If there are additional dimensions, then they might show up in the experimental data as deviations from the behavior of particles that are supposed to be there. Researchers at facilities such as the Large Hadron Collider (LHC) are looking for indirect evidence of extra dimensions by analyzing the behavior of particles when they are subjected to extremely high energy.

Observational Cosmology and the Cosmic Microwave Background: Observational cosmology offers an additional approach to the subject of exploring the signs of interdimensional physics. There is a possibility that the influence of other dimensions on the history of the cosmos could be shown by anomalies or patterns in the cosmic microwave background (CMB), which is the remainder of the radiation that was produced in the early universe. Information obtained through observations made by satellites such as the Planck observatory provides significant contributions to our understanding of the structure of the cosmos on a massive scale.

Experiments in Quantum Physics and Entanglement: Quantum physics experiments are continuing to investigate the nature of entanglement and the possible implications it may have for interdimensional interactions. It is possible that the boundaries of non-locality can be tested, and that the behavior of entangled particles can be studied under controlled settings.

This could provide clues to the fundamental fabric of reality, which could potentially transcend our conventional conception of space and time.

Astrophysical events and Gravity Waves: The field of astroparticle physics is concerned with the study of cosmic events that may be affected by the existence of additional dimensions to the universe. Gravity waves, which are ripples in spacetime that are created by huge cosmic events, offer a potential avenue for detecting the effects of other dimensions. It is the intention of future observatories, such as the Laser Interferometer Space Antenna (LISA), to investigate gravity waves and the possible connection that they have with interdimensional physics.

Conflicts & Difficulties to Overcome:

Experimental Restrictions and Energy Scales The experimental investigation of interdimensional physics is confronted with a number of severe challenges, one of which is the requirement for extremely high energy scales, which may be beyond the capabilities of the technology that is currently available. Furthermore, theoretical constructions such as extra dimensions or branes may appear at energy levels that are substantially higher than those that are possible in particle accelerators of the present day, which makes it difficult to directly validate these entities through experimentation.

Consistency with Observational Data: In order to be consistent with observational data and known physical processes, theoretical frameworks that propose interdimensional physics need to demonstrate consistency. It is possible that the validity of these theories could be called into question due to inconsistencies or conflicts with experimental data, despite the fact that they provide elegant answers to particular issues in physics. In the subject of study, one of the most important aspects of continuing disputes is the contradiction that exists between theoretical elegance and empirical validity.

The role of the observer in quantum mechanics presents a number of philosophical and interpretive issues. Quantum measurement and observer effects are two examples of these challenges. There is a school of thought that proposes that the act of measurement or observation has the potential to collapse wavefunctions and have an effect on the nature of reality. Within the realm of interdimensional physics, the topic of how to comprehend the connection that exists between awareness, observation, and the fundamental nature of reality continues to be a matter of debate and a source of uncertainty.

When pondering the potential repercussions of altering or accessing other dimensions, the investigation of interdimensional physics raises ethical and metaphysical questions. This is especially true when one considers the potential ramifications of such an action.

Complex concerns that go beyond the scope of scientific research are raised when people talk about the impact that interdimensional technologies have on consciousness, the nature of existence, and the ethical implications of these technologies.

Possible Consequences and Considerations:

Applications in Technology: In the not too distant future, theoretical developments in interdimensional physics may lead to technology applications that go beyond our current grasp of the subject matter. It is possible that innovative methods of space travel and exploration could be made possible through the utilization and stabilization of concepts such as wormholes. The ethical and practical issues that are linked with such technology, on the other hand, are enormous and require serious thought.

A Better Understanding of Dark Matter and Dark Energy Interdimensional physics has the potential to shed light on the nature of dark matter and dark energy, which are enigmatic components that constitute the majority of the mass-energy composition of the universe. It is possible that the existence of extra dimensions could provide explanations for the qualities of these cosmic occurrences that are difficult to explain, thereby giving insight on the underlying dynamics that control the universe.

Cosmic Inflation and the Early cosmos: Theory frameworks within the field of interdimensional physics contribute to our knowledge of cosmic inflation, which refers to the fast expansion of the cosmos in its early stages. The goal of physicists is to improve models of inflation and answer unanswered concerns regarding the uniformity and structure of the cosmic microwave background. This will be accomplished by taking into account the influence of extra dimensions or branes.

Speculations within the area of interdimensional physics transcend beyond the confines of conventional research, touching on important concerns about consciousness and the nature of reality. These new perspectives reveal that there are new ways of looking at the relationship between awareness and reality. There are ideas that suggest that there is a relationship between consciousness and the fabric of the cosmos. These theories suggest that the mind may play a significant part in determining the basic characteristics of existence.

Interdimensional physics is at the forefront of both scientific research and metaphysical inquiry due to the richness of its theoretical framework and the possibility that it is based on speculation. The pursuit of comprehending the existence of parallel universes, extra dimensions, and alternate realities stretches the boundaries of our existing understanding of the cosmos, despite the fact that it is firmly founded in established theories such as string theory and quantum physics.

String theory, brane theory, and the multiverse hypothesis are examples of theoretical frameworks that offer pathways for researching interdimensional physics. Each of these frameworks offers a unique perspective on the nature of reality. Despite the fact that they are confronted with significant obstacles, experimental efforts are still being made to investigate the fabric of spacetime in search of evidence of interdimensional events.

Despite the fact that academics are now navigating the theoretical landscape and experimental frontiers of interdimensional physics, the topic continues to be an intriguing arena for both scientific rigor and imaginative imagination. Beyond the sphere of physics, the consequences of unraveling the secrets of other dimensions touch on philosophical, ethical, and metaphysical questions that challenge our knowledge of the fundamental nature of the world. These considerations also test our ability to comprehend the underlying nature of the cosmos.

As part of the never-ending quest for knowledge, interdimensional physics encourages scientists, philosophers, and everyone with inquisitive minds to ponder the potential of realms that are beyond our perception as well as the fundamental interconnectivity of the universe. Our adventure to bridge the gap between worlds is unfolding as we continue to explore the undiscovered frontiers of theoretical physics. This trip is calling us to reevaluate the fundamental fabric of our existence as well as the mysteries that lay beyond the veil of our observable reality.

7.1 Expanding the scope to interdimensional physics and parallel universes

Our comprehension of the universe has been significantly expanded as a result of the investigation of interdimensional physics and parallel universes. This investigation, which is founded on sophisticated theoretical frameworks and pushes the frontiers of conventional science, takes us beyond the limitations of the cosmos that we can observe. The theoretical underpinnings of interdimensional physics, the idea of parallel universes, experimental concerns, and the broader ramifications for our perception of reality are all topics that are covered in depth in this extensive debate.

A Foundational Approach to Theory:

A theoretical framework that explains the fundamental building elements of the universe as microscopic, vibrating strings is known as string theory. This theory is at the forefront of interdimensional physics and is considered to be the most advanced theory in the field. In string theory, it is postulated that there are other dimensions available in addition to the three spatial dimensions that are commonly known. The compactification of these additional dimensions, which are frequently beyond our ability to observe, results in the introduction of a multidimensional landscape that stretches the fabric of space as we perceive it.

There are many different interpretations of quantum physics and cosmological theories, and these interpretations give rise to the multiverse theory. It postulates the presence of several worlds, each of which operates according to a different set of physical laws and parameters. It is possible that these worlds exist in parallel with our own or that they originate from the same cosmic origins. In the multiverse theory, each universe is a distinct iteration that possesses its own set of options and conditions. This enormous cosmic tapestry is offered as a result of the multiverse hypothesis.

Brane Theory and Parallel Dimensions: Brane theory, which is an extension of string theory, presents the idea of multidimensional structures that are referred to as "branes." The idea that our universe is a brane that exists in a space with greater dimensions is a well-known thought experiment. The existence of parallel dimensions on separate branes is a possibility, as is the possibility that cosmic occurrences are influenced by interactions between multiple branes. By utilizing this paradigm, one might have an interesting perspective from which to investigate the interconnection of various realities.

Quantum Entanglement and Non-Locality: Quantum entanglement, a process in which particles become associated in ways that defy classical ideas of locality, provides a clue at the potential links that exist across regions of space that are very far apart. Quantum entanglement, according to certain interpretations, may be able to extend beyond the confines of our observable reality, thereby offering a look into the interrelated nature of parallel realms.

The idea of parallel universes that exists:

Within the field of quantum mechanics, the Many-Worlds Interpretation claims that every quantum event results in the production of several, divergent realities. This interpretation is based on the idea that quantum mechanics gives rise to various realities. There is a distinct branch of the multiverse that is responsible for the realization of every conceivable consequence of a quantum event. Even though the Many-Worlds Interpretation is just one of many possible interpretations of quantum physics, it has garnered a lot of attention due to the implications it holds regarding the existence of an infinite number of parallel universes to consider.

The concept of bubble universes within the multiverse is supported by inflationary cosmology, which describes the fast expansion of the cosmos in its early stages. This provides a backdrop for the hypothesis that bubble universes exist within the multiverse. The production of bubble universes, each of which possesses its own unique set of physical attributes, could be the result of quantum fluctuations that occur during the process of cosmic inflation. The multiverse has a wide variety of bubble universes, each of which contributes to the richness of the possible cosmic situations.

Pocket Universes and the String Landscape The string landscape hypothesis proposes that the production of pocket universes is produced as a result of the vast number of conceivable configurations of fundamental constants and extra dimensions. The multiverse is characterized by its diversity, which is contributed to by the fact that each pocket world could appear with a unique set of physical rules and attributes. The concept of a large cosmic landscape that contains an infinite number of possible worlds is presented by the string landscape.

Parallel universes can also be conceived of as different realities that coexist with our own Earth. This is another way of thinking about parallel universes. It is possible that these realities are different from ours as a result of different historical occurrences, preferences, or quantum results. When it comes to the nature of choice and determinism across the multiverse, the idea of parallel Earths, which are places where recognizable landscapes and history unfold differently, captivates the imagination and raises issues about the structure of the universe.

Considerations Regarding the Experiment:

High-Energy Particle Physics: High-energy particle accelerators are frequently utilized in the course of experimental operations that are designed to investigate inter-dimensional physics. Both the detection of signatures of additional dimensions and the investigation of the veracity of string theory are the goals of these investigations. The hunt for particles that behave differently from what is predicted by traditional models provides vital insights into the theoretical frameworks that underpin interdimensional physics. This is despite the fact that direct proof of extra dimensions continues to be difficult.

Research Concerning the Cosmic Microwave Background (CMB):
A cosmology window into the probable effect of other dimensions can be found through observations of the cosmic microwave background (CMB), which is the remaining radiation from the early cosmos. The cosmic microwave background (CMB) may contain anomalies or patterns that are indicative of interactions with parallel worlds or characteristics of the multiverse. The Cosmic Microwave Background (CMB) is still being investigated by cutting-edge telescopes and observational instruments in search of hints on the nature of the origins of the universe.

Astrophysical Phenomena and Gravitational Waves: The study of gravitational waves, which is one example of an astrophysical phenomenon, offers opportunities to investigate the possibility of the effect of extra dimensions. The ripples in space-time that are created by large cosmic events are known as gravitational waves. These waves have the potential to carry information about the structure of space beyond the cosmos that we can observe. Experiments are now being conducted, including those that use gravitational wave detectors, with the purpose of determining the cosmological implications of interdimensional phenomena.

Quantum Experiments and Entanglement Studies Quantum experiments that concentrate on the composition of entanglement make a contribution to our comprehension of non-locality and the possible links that exist across parallel dimensions. By manipulating quantum states and investigating the entanglement of particles, experiments are conducted with the intention of gaining basic insights into the fabric of reality. These experiments aim to go beyond the traditional concepts of space and independence.

Conflicts & Difficulties to Overcome:
One of the most significant obstacles in the field of interdimensional physics is the difficulty of gaining access to higher-dimensional phenomena through experimentation. Energy constraints are another difficulty that must be overcome. It is possible that the energy scales that are necessary to witness the impacts of branes or to manifest more dimensions are beyond the limits of the technology that is currently available. Theoretical frameworks that attempt to anticipate such occurrences frequently include energy levels that are higher than those that can be achieved by modern particle accelerators.

Consistency with Existing Physics Theoretical constructs within the field of interdimensional physics need to be consistent with the existing principles of physics and the facts obtained from observations. Although these theories provide elegant solutions to particular issues, the validity of these ideas may be called into question due to inconsistencies or conflicts with the outcomes of empirical research. In this area of study, one of the most persistent challenges is learning how to strike a compromise between theoretical elegance and experimental verification.

The role of the observer in quantum mechanics presents a number of philosophical and interpretive issues. Quantum measurement and observer effects are two examples of these challenges. As a result of the fact that the act of measurement or observation has the potential to affect the outcomes of quantum events, issues are raised regarding the nature of reality and the role that the observer plays in forming the quantum landscape. In addition to these issues, there are also discussions about the role that the observer plays in shaping the nature of parallel universes.

Ethical and Metaphysical Implications The pursuit of interdimensional physics poses ethical and metaphysical questions, particularly when pondering the potential repercussions of accessing or manipulating other dimensions. This is especially true when those effects are taken into account. In the course of conversations concerning the nature of consciousness, the influence on individual experience, and the ethical limitations of interdimensional investigation, significant reflections on the ramifications of such activities are prompted.

Possible Consequences and Considerations:

Possibilities in Technology: If interdimensional physics were to be exploited and understood in more depth, it could have the potential to open the door to revolutionary technological possibilities. In the event that they are stabilized, concepts such as traversable wormholes have the potential to open up new entry points for space travel and exploration. However, careful attention is required because of the ethical, theoretical, and practical issues that are linked with such technology.

Insights into the Cosmology of the Universe The investigation of the nature of parallel universes and extra dimensions offers cosmologists new views on fundamental topics. It's possible that the presence of a multiverse could provide answers to some of the riddles of the universe, such as dark matter and dark energy as well. In order to shed light on the evolution of the universe on both the cosmic and quantum scales, it would be helpful to have an understanding of the interconnection of parallel realms.

Interdimensional physics challenges us to grapple with important philosophical problems concerning the nature of reality, awareness, and existence. These concerns are a result of the research of interdimensional physics. There are philosophical reckonings that go beyond the limitations of empirical research that are prompted by speculations about the interconnection of parallel dimensions. There is a rich tapestry of philosophical inquiry that is stimulated by conversations concerning the nature of choice, determinism, and the role of the observer in producing reality.

Reimagining Space and Time The field of interdimensional physics presents a challenge to our traditional view of space and time, prompting us to rethink the fundamental structure of the world. When we consider the potential of parallel universes, we are presented with the idea that time and space may unfold in ways that are external to our conscious knowledge. As a result of this paradigm shift, our preconceived notions about the nature of existence and the order of the cosmos are being called into question.

An intriguing investigation that lies at the crossroads of theoretical physics, experimental investigation, and philosophical reflection is represented by the trip into interdimensional physics and parallel universes. The bounds of our understanding of the universe are being pushed farther by this discipline, which has its origins in theoretical frameworks such as string theory, brane theory, and the multiverse hypothesis.

As scientists explore the theoretical landscapes and practical boundaries of interdimensional physics, issues concerning the nature of reality, the fabric of the cosmos, and the interconnection of parallel dimensions are brought to the forefront of their minds.

The difficulties, debates, and ethical concerns that are linked with this exploration highlight the difficulty of deciphering the mysteries that exist beyond the observable cosmos that we are now experiencing.

Although interdimensional physics is still considered to be a theoretical and speculative field, the consequences of its investigation reach into the fields of technology, cosmology, philosophy, and our fundamental comprehension of what it means to be alive. Scientists, thinkers, and explorers are being beckoned to continue their adventure into the unknown by the quest to widen the scope to include interdimensional physics and parallel worlds. This voyage is calling us to contemplate the immense possibilities that may lie beyond the curtain of our observable reality.

7.2 Examining theories of dimensional overlap and ghostly interactions

Those who are interested in the domain of paranormal occurrences frequently have the opportunity to interact with entities that are popularly known as ghosts or spirits. Numerous hypotheses have surfaced in an effort to provide an explanation for the nature of ghostly contacts as researchers continue to dive deeper into the mysteries surrounding these spectral experiences. Theories of dimensional overlap, which propose that ghosts can live in dimensions that interact with our own, are a fascinating field of investigation that could be pursued. An in-depth investigation into the theories that propose dimensional overlap, the possible mechanisms that are responsible for ghostly interactions, and the ramifications for our comprehension of the supernatural are all included in this exhaustive examination.

Different dimensions overlap theories include:

A growing number of theoretical physicists are beginning to acknowledge the existence of multidimensional frameworks, which are frameworks that extend beyond the traditional three spatial dimensions. A number of theoretical frameworks, such as string theory, postulate the presence of additional dimensions that may be compressed or concealed from our ordinary perception. Dimensional overlap theories believe that beings, such as ghosts, could exist in dimensions that intersect with our own, hence allowing for contact between the two realms on occasion. These theories are based on the principle that dimensional overlap exists.

Parallel worlds and Multiverse Theories: The concept of parallel worlds, which is frequently investigated within the context of multiverse theories, postulates the presence of several realities that coexist with one another. Within the scope of this discussion, ghosts may be entities that originate from parallel universes that intersect with our own. There is a possibility that the barriers between these worlds are porous, which provides the opportunity for fleeting interactions and manifestations that challenge our conventional understanding of space and reality.

Interconnected Realms and String Landscape: The string landscape hypothesis, which is a part of string theory, is the one that presents the concept of pocket universes or interconnected realms. There is a possibility that every pocket universe has its own unique set of physical laws and conditions. In accordance with this hypothesis, ghostly interactions may take place when the borders that separate these interrelated realms briefly break, enabling entities to travel between dimensions.

Brane Theory and Entities on Branes: Brane theory, which is an extension of string theory, includes multidimensional structures that are referred to as "branes." This brane is thought to exist in a realm with higher dimensions, and our universe is regarded to be one of them. It has been hypothesized that these brains are home to a variety of entities, including ghosts. The interactions that take place between the various brains have the potential to result in the appearance of ghosts in our observable reality.

Methods by Which Ghostly Interactions Take Place:

Non-Locality and Quantum Entanglement: The phenomena of quantum entanglement, in which particles become coupled in ways that defy classical concepts of locality, is frequently invoked in theories of ghostly interactions. Quantum entanglement may also be referred to as non-locality. It is possible that quantum entanglement could permit non-local connections, which would allow for the manifestation of ghostly events in our observable world. This would be the case if entities exist in dimensions that are beyond our own.

Imprints and Residual Energy: There are ideas that suggest ghosts could be imprints of residual energy that were left behind by traumatic or intensely emotional experiences. In this hypothetical situation, these imprints might be present in dimensions that are not our own, and under certain circumstances, they would start to resonate with our reality, which would result in the appearance of ghostly apparitions or manifestations.

Time-Space Anomalies: Theories of dimensional overlap frequently take into consideration the possibility of time-space anomalies, which are characterized by the blurring of the boundaries between several dimensions. When these anomalies produce windows or portals through which entities from other dimensions can briefly pass into our own, it is possible that ghostly exchanges will take place.

Intentional Interaction and Consciousness The role of consciousness in theories of dimensional overlap argues that entities, including ghosts, may possess a sort of consciousness that permits them to interact with one another in a deliberate manner. Consciousness has the potential to serve as a conduit between different dimensions, enabling entities to materialize or speak with persons in our respective realities.

Accounts of anecdotal evidence and evidence:

Anecdotal tales of ghostly experiences frequently involve descriptions of entities that abruptly appear, vanish, or present in ways that violate the rules of physics as we understand them. Eyewitness accounts are also known as first-hand accounts. Testimonies from eyewitnesses constitute a significant portion of the evidence that lends support to theories of dimensional overlap. These testimonies include persons who have reported encounters that are consistent with the processes that have been postulated to explain ghostly phenomena.

Electronic Voice Phenomena (EVP): The study of Electronic Voice Phenomena (EVP) includes capturing inexplicable voices or noises on audio recording equipment. Some academics believe that electronic voice phenomena (EVP) could be evidence that beings are communicating from dimensions that are not our own. It is believed that these strange sounds, which are frequently inaudible in real time, reveal themselves during particular recording sessions, which suggests that they are the result of intentional engagement.

Evidence in the Form of Photographs and films: Photographs and films that capture apparitions, shadow figures, or light abnormalities that cannot be explained are regularly presented as evidence of ghostly interactions. While skeptics frequently ascribe such visual events to camera artifacts or natural explanations, proponents of dimensional overlap theories suggest that these images could represent beings briefly crossing into our reality. dimensional overlap theories provide an explanation for the phenomenon.

Activity of the Poltergeist: Poltergeist activity, which is characterized by inexplicable physical disturbances such as the movement of objects, sounds, or even physical attacks, is sometimes tied to notions of dimensional overlap. The theory that beings from other dimensions may exert influence on our reality under certain conditions is consistent with the poltergeist phenomenon, which is characterized by its seemingly spontaneous and unpredictable nature.

Skepticism and Obstacles on the Path:
Lack of Reproducible Evidence The absence of evidence that can be reproduced is one of the most significant obstacles that theoretical frameworks of dimensional overlap encounter in the field of research on paranormal occurrences. As a result of the fact that many ghostly encounters are based on personal experiences and anecdotal descriptions, it is challenging to create a scientific foundation for the mechanisms of dimensional contact that have been postulated.

Skeptics contend that many of the experiences that are attributed to ghostly contacts can be explained by natural or psychological reasons due to the fact that they are alternative explanations.

The tendency to discern significant patterns in random stimuli, also known as pareidolia, as well as cognitive biases, may be factors that contribute to the incorrect interpretation of everyday occurrences as being paranormal. A number of other hypotheses continue to be feasible in the absence of rigorous scientific data.

There are issues associated with recording definitive proof of dimensions overlap due to the limitations of the technology that is currently available. When conducting investigations into the paranormal, it is common practice to make use of technologies such as electronic voice phenomena (EVP) recording devices and infrared cameras. However, the interpretation of the data that is captured frequently depends on subjective analysis, which leaves space for skepticism regarding the authenticity of the evidence.

Technique in the Scientific Field Some people believe that the scientific technique that is used in the field of paranormal research is not always considered rigorous enough. When it comes to demonstrating the legitimacy of dimensional overlap hypotheses, controlled tests, studies that have been reviewed by peers, and strict adherence to scientific protocols are all key components. There is a lack of agreement among members of the scientific community, which makes it difficult for these theories to gain wider recognition.

Possible Consequences and Considerations:

Theories of dimensional overlap present a challenge to the conventional notions of consciousness and its connection to the fabric of reality. This presents an opportunity for reinterpreting the nature of human consciousness. It is necessary to reevaluate the nature of consciousness and the function it plays in determining the dynamics that exist between dimensions if it is discovered that entities from other dimensions possess a form of consciousness that enables them to interact deliberately with one another.

Technology Developments in the Field of Paranormal research The research of dimensional overlap theories has the potential to promote technological developments in the field of paranormal investigation. It is possible that the scientific rigor of paranormal research could be improved by the development of improved instruments that are capable of detecting small energy fluctuations, disturbances in spacetime, or abnormalities linked with other dimensions.

The acceptance of dimensional overlap theories would have significant repercussions for both culture and philosophy. These repercussions would be substantial. The traditional religious and spiritual interpretations of the afterlife would be called into question, and alternative explanations for ghostly phenomena would be offered. It is possible that this shift in perspective will cause social views regarding the nature of existence and the continuity of awareness to undergo a transformation.

Ethical Considerations In the event that dimensional overlap ideas are accepted by a wider audience, ethical questions will arise concerning the purposeful interaction with entities that possess dimensions that are different from our own. For the purpose of conducting investigations and explorations of the paranormal, ethical rules would be required because of the questions that arise regarding the rights, intentions, and potential implications of such interactions.

The investigation of ideas that propose dimensional overlap and interactions between ghosts takes us into a domain where the borders of our understanding of reality become more hazy. Even if these theories provide compelling explanations for paranormal experiences, there are still many obstacles to overcome in order to establish empirical proof and reach a consensus among members of the scientific community around these hypotheses.

In the realm of hypotheses about dimensional overlap, the corpus of knowledge is enriched by the anecdotal stories, electronic recordings, and photographic evidence that are associated with ghostly encounters. Skepticism, on the other hand, is widespread, and the scientific community insists that these theories be validated by the use of rigorous methods and reproducibility.

As the investigation into the nature of ghostly encounters continues, the idea of dimensional overlap continues to be an intriguing one that calls for additional investigation and investigation. There is still a question that has to be answered regarding whether or not these ideas will transform our knowledge of consciousness, the fabric of reality, and the mysteries of the afterlife. This question is currently awaiting empirical inspection and the evolution of technology in order to unveil the secrets that may lie beyond the curtain that separates the dimensions.

7.3 Concluding insights on the potential scientific understanding of the spirit realm

In the perspective of scientific investigation, the investigation of the spirit realm provides a task that is both difficult and multifaceted. Throughout the course of this conversation, we have explored a number of different theories, some of which provide dimensional overlap, others propose multiverse hypotheses, and yet others propose quantum entanglement, all with the intention of providing possible causes for ghostly encounters. As we come to the end of this investigation, a number of significant realizations and factors come to light, which shed light on the ever-changing landscape of scientific understanding concerning the spirit realm.

Conversations Between Disciplines The junction of the supernatural and scientific investigation calls for a conversation between different fields of study that goes beyond the boundaries of traditional disciplines.

Although physics, psychology, and philosophy each bring their own distinct points of view to the table, the intricacies of the spirit realm necessitate the creation of joint initiatives that incorporate a variety of approaches and conceptual frameworks. These kind of multidisciplinary approaches aid in the development of a more all-encompassing comprehension of the phenomena that are related with the spirit realm.

The possible scientific understanding of the spirit realm must prioritize empirical rigor and respect to the scientific process. This is because of the importance of doing research in accordance with scientific principles. The scientific validity of suggested theories must be established through rigorous experiments, controlled studies, and reproducibility. Although anecdotal experiences, eyewitness testimonials, and inquiries into the paranormal all contribute to the body of knowledge, these are not sufficient to demonstrate the validity of proposed theories. It is absolutely necessary to make technological and methodological advancements in order to bring the field of paranormal research up to the level of scientific legitimacy.

The search of understanding the spirit realm raises ethical problems, particularly with regard to human experiences and the potential repercussions of purposeful encounters with entities from other dimensions. These considerations are brought up as a result of the pursuit of this understanding. It is necessary for the area of paranormal research to establish ethical principles in order to address concerns regarding the protection of individuals' privacy, the provision of informed consent, and the well-being of those who are involved in investigations. In order to successfully navigate the ethical landscape of paranormal investigation, it is of the utmost importance to respect the subjective nature of human experiences and cultural interpretations respectively.

The incorporation of consciousness studies brings an intriguing new facet to the investigation, which is the function that consciousness plays in notions of the spirit realm. A significant contribution to the understanding of the subjective experiences that are linked with ghostly encounters is made by the field of consciousness studies, which encompasses the fields of neuroscience, psychology, and philosophy. Within the realm of scientific inquiry, the investigation of the nature of consciousness and its possible connection to the fabric of reality provides a bridge between the rich tapestry of human experience and the realm of scientific inquiry.

Technological Developments and Tools for Investigating the Paranormal The ongoing development of technology has the potential to bring about a revolution in the methodology of paranormal investigations.

It is possible that improved technologies that are able to detect minor energy fluctuations, disturbances in spacetime, or abnormalities connected with other dimensions could give empirical data that either supports or refutes the ideas that are now in contention. The incorporation of cutting-edge technology into the investigation of the paranormal not only adds to the scientific rigor of the area but also offers new paths for investigation.

Recognizing the cultural diversity of interpretations and beliefs around the spirit realm is essential to creating tolerance within scientific discourse. This is because of the importance of cultural sensitivity and diversity. There are numerous cultural, theological, and spiritual viewpoints that each provide their own distinct glasses through which the spirit realm can be comprehended. This diversity should be embraced since it contributes to the enrichment of the conversation and supports a more holistic approach to investigating the mysteries of the paranormal.

Inquiry with an Open Mind and Skepticism: When navigating the complexities of the spirit realm, it is vital to strike a balance between investigating with an open mind and maintaining a healthy dosage of skepticism. A critical evaluation of the data and a commitment to scientific inspection guarantee that the search of understanding remains a grounded and objective perspective. This involves keeping open to new possibilities and alternative explanations, while also maintaining an openness to new possibilities. It is possible to use skepticism as a beneficial catalyst for the refinement of theories and approaches if it is treated with intellectual honesty.

Potential for Paradigm transformations The idea of a scientific understanding of the spirit dimension carries with it the interesting possibility of paradigm transformations within the frameworks of both the scientific community and the cultural community. There is a possibility that the boundaries of our current understanding will extend as new evidence is discovered and theories continue to develop. This will present a challenge to our preconceived notions regarding the nature of reality, consciousness, and the afterlife. One of the most important factors in fostering a dynamic and progressive approach to scientific discovery is a readiness to welcome paradigm shifts.

The scientific study of the spirit realm continues to be a field that is constantly growing and dynamic, and it continues to require an approach that is nuanced and balanced. In spite of the fact that theories that propose dimensional overlap and ghostly interactions present exciting prospects, the way forward requires a dedication to scientific rigor, collaboration across disciplines, and ethical considerations. In order to conduct a comprehensive investigation into the mysteries that surround the spirit realm, it is necessary to incorporate developments in technology, studies of consciousness, and a respect for the diversity of cultural traditions.

It is important to exercise care and curiosity as one embarks on the quest of gaining a scientific understanding of the spirit realm. The book encourages researchers, academics, and enthusiasts to explore the unexplored regions of the paranormal by employing a combination of intellectual rigor, open-minded inquiry, and a profound understanding for the diverse range of human experiences. The merger of science and the unexplained has the possibility of expanding our comprehension of the cosmos and the intricate tapestry of existence. Even as we continue to investigate the mysteries of the spirit realm, this convergence holds the promise of expanding our understanding.

www.ingramcontent.com/pod-product-compliance
Lightning Source LLC
LaVergne TN
LVHW010645200726
843507LV00011B/1766